# THE Book on Personal Transformation

*7 simple steps to
becoming an outrageously successful NEW YOU*

**Peter J Green**

First published in 2012

Copyright © 2012 Peter Green

The right of Peter Green to be identified as the author of this work has been asserted in accordance with sections 77 and 78 of the Copyright Designs and Patents Act 1988

ISBN-13: 978-1481060202

ISBN-10: 1481060201

Illustrations by John Daryl D. Obera

Cover design by KL Designs

All rights reserved. No part of this work may be reproduced in any material form (including photocopying or storing in any medium by electronic means and whether or not transiently or incidentally to some other use of this publication) without the written permission of the copyright holder.

www.petergreenintl.com

www.nowtransform.com

Disclaimer

The author asserts that he cannot be held liable or responsible for the outcomes of decisions the reader makes as a result of reading this book. The reader is wholly responsible for their actions and should seek relevant professional advice before making a decision that may affect their life.

To my family.

You are my pride and joy,
you give me constant inspiration and happiness.

Life is too short to let anything get in the way.

Aim for the stars and you might just hit the moon!

Mum, Dad, Anna, Mamma, Rob, Becky, Rick, Jennifer, James Carlie, Sharona, Butch, Dan, Cat, Lucy, Jules, Thomas, Amy, , David, Kathy.

Live Well,
Laugh Often,
Love Each Other,
and Above All,
Be True to the Real You.

Peter has written a thought provoking and empowering book. "*THE Book on Personal Transformation.*"

He has taken what can be a complex, daunting and sometimes mystifying subject and broken it down into realistic, easy to follow, no nonsense steps.

Importantly he ensures you remain authentically you, (no pretending to be someone else), while becoming an amazing NEW YOU.

He inspires you, challenges you and coaches you with his unique style and humour to reinvent yourself.

Whether you just want to tweak something or make a complete change this excellent book is for you, I highly recommend it.

**Hannah Jones -**
Leader of Learning
**www.BlueKiteCoach.com**


One thing that's for sure is we are ALL capable of being and achieving more than we believe possible. The sad truth is that most people never do anything about it and pass through this life achieving at best mediocrity.

Having previously experienced personal transformation and now having helped thousands of people achieve great things myself, this book, "*THE Book on Personal Transformation*" by Peter Green, really resonated with me.

Peter draws on his experience, research and knowledge to inspire, cajole, guide and coach you through his excellent process for change and personal reinvention.

I urge you to read this book and follow his guidance with commitment and courage, I'm sure you will be delighted with the successful New You that emerges.

A quotation that Peter uses sums it up "*Life isn't about finding yourself, it's about creating yourself*" – George Bernard Shaw

**Raymond Aaron –**
NY Times Best Selling Author
www.UltimateAuthorBootcamp.com

# Contents

| | | |
|---|---|---|
| | Preamble | 1 |
| | Introduction – Why You Must Break Out of Your Jail | 5 |
| 1 | What's Lurking in Your Attic? It's Time for a Clear Out | 16 |
| 2 | Set Sail on Your Voyage of Discovery - Explore, Dream, Discover | 29 |
| 3 | Unleash Your Leonardo Da Vinci and Create Your Masterpiece | 38 |
| 4 | Let The Butterfly Emerge - Time to Act Like You Belong | 45 |
| 5 | Roll Call! Identify the Sappers and the Zappers | 61 |
| 6 | The Perfect Refinement | 69 |
| 7 | Onwards and Upwards | 77 |
| | The Final Word | 89 |
| | A Note from the Author | 90 |

# ACKNOWLEDGEMENTS

Thanks to everyone who encouraged and helped me with this book.

A huge thank you to my ever-loving, but long suffering, beautiful wife, Anna, who continues to support me and also keeps me in check while I flit around keeping all the plates of my big ideas and dreams spinning.

To my good friend and coaching buddy, Hannah Jones, for the powerful questions that spurred me along, coaxed me out of my phases of procrastination and helped clear my thinking.

To my excellent editor, Sally Salvati, for perfectly capturing my voice and message, while remaining flexible to my requests.

To Kathi, of KL Designs, for a stunning cover design, and to all those who helped in the selection process.

To my good friend, Dave Hyner, for being such a great bloke and inspiring me to set some massive goals.

Finally to Raymond Aaron for giving me the methods, systems, guidance and inside knowledge to write this book.

# FOREWORD

Many of us have something or many things we want to change about ourselves, but feel it is either too difficult or worse, impossible.

One day we might get a painful wakeup call that propels us reluctantly into a change process, only to emerge astounded at the successful new "YOU" that's been created. I should know; it happened to me.

But you don't have to wait for that painful wakeup call. In this book, *"THE Book on Personal Transformation"*, Peter Green provides you with an early wakeup call followed by a fast track and thorough method for creating the New You.

Through his research, insight and personal experience, Peter has cleverly distilled down the process of personal reinvention into a series of realistic and practical steps.

We only have one life, but as Peter says, *"It's never too late to become the person you were meant to be"*.

You control who you are and your destiny; make sure you grasp that control with both hands and use this book to become outrageously successful.

Raymond Aaron –
NY Times Best Selling Author
www.UltimateAuthorBootcamp.com

# PREAMBLE

Your reinvention may be prompted by a defining event: divorce, illness, some kind of wakeup call (a metaphorical slap in the face); or it may be that you are just feeling a little stagnant at your current point in life. Let's face it... sometimes we just need to give our life a bit of a 'shake up' to prevent it from going stale.

Whatever your motivation, this book will help you take a close look at YOU - who you have become and more importantly who you want to become.

The simple fact that you are even reading this book means something has resonated within you and more importantly you have the spark or desire to consider doing something about it, and that's exactly what I am going to tap into and work with.

I know this might seem to be a little far-fetched, but I can assure you that if you put your mind to it you can achieve personal change and become more successful.

This book will help you **'become the person you were meant to be'**.

As your personal coach throughout this book, I will be making a couple of assumptions: I will assume you are generally well and are both mentally and emotionally strong. If this is not the case, maybe you should stop reading now and wait until you are in a better place before continuing.

I have high expectations of everyone I coach, including you. I will guide you through my missions and reflections, supplying you with tools and suggestions to give you the best possible chance of success.

All I ask of you in return is total honesty and commitment.

Within the pages of this book you will find world class coaching and proven methods of personal transformation, but there is only one person who can really make your reinvention work and that is YOU. It's your change, no one else's, and you must take responsibility, fully own it and commit to seeing it through to the very end.

I promise I will be with you every step of the way, supporting and encouraging your progress, but ultimately it is you who holds the key to your success. I'll help you discover it; your job is to use it and not lose it.

During this journey I will be asking you to carry out various self-discovery missions, make notes and compile lists. I suggest you treat yourself to a new notebook just for this purpose. Not a flimsy paperback, but a quality hardback book that you can keep. Give it a name that means something to you, like 'My New Life' or 'The New Me', whatever works for you.

## New Roles for You

I have some new roles for you; well they are not completely new, just new to you.

I want you for a moment to imagine you are going to make a movie.

The project you will be working on is titled 'The New You'.

You don't need to recruit lots of people because this movie is about you. For the whole of this book, for the entire duration of this project and in fact for the rest of your life, you are going to become a writer, a director, a producer and a star.

You don't need anyone to play the lead role, because you are the star.

You don't need to hire a writer, because guess what, you are also the writer - think about it, who else is as well-qualified? Who knows more than anyone else about what you want to happen in this movie?

You don't need to hire a director, because when it comes down to deciding how each scene should play out, well the best person once again would be you, wouldn't it?

When it comes to making movies, it's fair to say that control of how the movie is made is shared between the writer, director, producer and main character. They control what happens, how it happens, and how it all plays out in the end.

That's exactly the level of control you have over how your life turns out.

This may sound fanciful but let me assure you it's the absolute truth.

From now on I want you to assume these roles and carry them out to the best of your ability in everything you do; you are in charge... of everything. It's ALL totally up to you!

Now, if all that sounds a bit scary to you, then good! It means you are taking this seriously and by doing so you have just increased your chances of success by 100%.

Next I want you to take those sensations of feeling scared and reinterpret them in your mind, because believe it or not, we experience exactly the same feelings when we are about to do something positive, fun and exciting. The difference is that we have programmed ourselves to interpret these feelings differently on account of what we perceive to be coming next! Remember... YOU are in control and you can now decide to interpret them differently.

## Quantum Energy, the Universe and the Law of Attraction

Since the explosive success of the book "The Secret", there has been so much written about this subject and I am certainly not going to attempt to cover it all here, but I do want to mention a few words in relation to personal change and success.

For those of you that may not be aware of this subject, here's a brief summary.

Scientists studying the most minute particles of matter have discovered that at the smallest level known to man (and I am talking very, very, very small) everything is made of the same stuff - that's you, me, trees, rocks, water etc., etc. In fact the whole universe is made up of these same particles. What's even more startling is that these particles are nothing more than raw energy vibrating at different frequencies. Even more amazing is that these particles of energy or matter are never stationary; they continuously flit around the universe. Even our thoughts are small bursts of energy that radiate out into the universe.

Even more interesting is the belief that everything in the known universe is interconnected at a quantum level, like a huge web or net, sometimes referred to as 'the super consciousness'.

All this scientific information leads to the conjecture that things can be manifested through thought - what an amazing concept!

Now we all know that you can't just dream of success, lie back and wait for it to happen. However, what it does indicate is that although we still need to take action and do things to achieve what we want in life, our thoughts probably have a much more significant impact on our chances of success than we ever realised.

# INTRODUCTION: The Great Escape - Why You Must Break Out of Your Jail

*"Whatever the mind can conceive and believe, the mind can achieve."*

Napoleon Hill

I am really glad you're reading this, because it means you are serious about changing your life for the better. Your specific reason for wanting to change is personal to you; how you go about the change, now that is something I can help you with.

Let's start with a couple of quotes that may help stimulate some action, both are poignant and sobering, but make incredibly valid points. The first is by Fiona Harrold: "*The greatest tragedy of a lifetime must be to live with regret, to reach a point when you are confronted with all the things you have not done or even tried.*" Then Paul Coelho states: "*One day you will wake up and there won't be any more time to do the things you always wanted to do*"

I appreciate the concept of personal transformation can be a bit scary, but it does not have to be. You may be thinking "I don't need to transform", but let me ask you this question "Are you really happy with everything you have right now? Are you really happy with the results you are getting in your life and/or business?"

Consider the title of this chapter "The great escape - why you must break out of your jail." This was no accident, it was chosen for a reason. Most of us are locked in to our current situation, our current way of being. At least that's how we act and sometimes what we believe. In reality the only bars you have at the windows and doors of your cell are the ones you put there yourself, the obstacles and blocks you constantly create in your life in terms of what you believe is possible.

As difficult as this may be to swallow, I have some bad news for you - all the results you are achieving right now and everything that you've had/done in your life up to now is completely your responsibility, totally due to who you are and who you have become. Now I don't want to hear your reasons why you believe that isn't true at the moment in your life. My goal with this book is to show you that it is true and more importantly, that it doesn't have to stay that way.

If you want different results in life, if you want different outcomes, then the only possible way you can achieve them is for you to change. I can hear you already saying "Well I can't change. I'm me and that's it! I can't be someone else."

I am not suggesting that you become someone else entirely; instead I'm suggesting that you find the real you - the best and most authentic part of who you are.

You see the beauty of the human being (or being human) is that nothing is permanent, not even you. The miracle of life is also the miracle of change when YOU change, everything else also changes.

And the greatest awareness of all you can have as stated by George Eliot is *"It's never too late to be who you might have been"*. My interpretation of that is *"It's never too late to become the person you were meant to be"*.

My commitment to you is that I will take you on an incredible journey; we will have an incredible adventure together. We are going to break open those bars on the cell windows of who you are now, and transform you and your life into the most outrageously successful life that you can dream of. I'm going to help you grow your self-belief to such a high level that you will be able to do and achieve anything.

You see one of my beliefs in life is that everybody has the same incredible potential inside of them - the potential to have and to be whatever you want to have and to be.

But the other promise I will make you is that this isn't going to be easy. The title of the book says that you can do it in seven simple steps - I can confirm that they are simple, but they're definitely not easy! It's going to take courage, commitment and real determination on your part, but I can promise you that I'll be there along the way with this book to help you reach your goal.

In order to make this project a success there are some commitments I need from you. The first is a high enough level of motivation. Do you really want this change? How much do want it? How badly do you want to get away from where you are at the moment? I'll help you reach for that motivation, but true motivation comes from the inside. I need your promise that you will reach deep inside yourself to grab that motivation.

Secondly I need you to do what needs to be done. Change is never comfortable. Our brains are actually programmed to make us feel uncomfortable through change as a safety mechanism, which is why many people never really achieve true change. I don't want you to be one of those people, because I know you can achieve more. However, you need to be aware that you may need to ramp up the self-discipline level to be able to reach your goal.

Thirdly, I need you to commit to believe in yourself. You may already have a high level of self-belief, in which case for this change process to work, all I need you to do is commit to continually increase it.

And fourthly you have to be prepared to challenge, because without an open mind and the ability to challenge what you already know or have, you can never move forward. To quote Einstein *"The problems that we face today cannot be solved by the same level of thinking that created them"*, which I think is a wonderful way of saying we have to challenge what we already believe to be true in order to move forward. All I ask of you is to be prepared to keep an open mind and be ready to challenge what you already know or have.

Now there is also some amazing science that underpins the basis of this journey that we will go on together. In recent decades there have been incredible advancements in the understanding of our brain, how it works and what it is capable of.

Scientists have created a new word for the discoveries they've made, which is very relevant to what we will be talking about. The word I'm referring to is 'neuroplasticity', which refers to the fact that scientists discovered the brain is not as fixed as we thought it was.

**Definition:** Neuroplasticity (from neural - pertaining to the nerves and/or brain and plastic - mouldable or changeable in structure) refers to changes in neural pathways and synapses which are due to changes in behaviour, environment and neural processes, as well as changes resulting from bodily injury. Neuroplasticity has replaced the formerly-held position that the brain is a physiologically static organ,

The 'old' belief was that once you reached your mid-20s, your brain growth was stable and complete in terms of its development and after that it was assumed to slowly and continuously degrade until death.

With the discovery of neuroplasticity, that line of thinking has all been turned on its head. Scientists have discovered a 'new' theory that our brains have the ability to do two things: to grow new neurons, so the brain can continue growing as long as it's stimulated and active; and the even more exciting discovery that the brain can effectively rewire itself.

Sometimes it happens after injury, which is where a lot of these discoveries have originated from. But amazingly they have discovered that it doesn't need to be as a result of suffering an injury. It appears we can actually choose to reprogram our brains so they act and operate differently - effectively re-programming and re-wiring our brains.

There a couple of examples I want to bring to your attention, which support this theory:

In 1969 brain scientist Paul Bach-y-Rita conducted a ground-breaking experiment that proved neuroplasticity existed. He managed to allow a blind person to see by taking the output of a video camera and connecting it to a special metallic grid, which was then attached to the blind person's tongue. The visual images from the camera were converted into electrical impulses, which in turn stimulated the senses on the blind person's tongue.

Their brain was then able to learn those stimulations and interpret them as images by routing the signals to the part of the brain that processes sight. The brain was effectively rewiring itself to stop using the old and damaged sight circuitry and start using alternative circuitry for the purpose of seeing.

That ground-breaking work has continued and today there are many blind or partially-sighted people, who are able to have basic vision using the modern day equivalent of Bach-y-Rita's equipment, called 'brain port'.

The second example draws on experiments conducted by NASA scientists on astronauts in preparation for space flight.

One of the problems with space flight was that astronauts were effectively confined in small spaces for long periods and due to weightlessness, they would often be viewing things upside down for long periods, which created disorientation. NASA wanted to simulate this environment to monitor how it affected the human body.

During training, a group of astronauts were locked in a small living pod and made to wear special convex goggles. These goggles presented the astronauts with a view that was flipped by 180°, in other words they saw everything upside down. They were made to wear these goggles all the time, including when sleeping.

The experiment was providing NASA with useful data until on about day 21 when one of the astronauts reported a malfunction with his goggles. He reported that they had stopped showing the view upside down.

What happened next stunned everyone. When they went to fix his goggles they found there was nothing wrong with them; they were still showing an image upside down, but the astronaut was now seeing everything the right way up!

The conclusion drawn was that his brain had re-wired itself with new neural pathways, so that it could present the image the correct way up in the astronaut's head.

Over the next few days, all the astronauts began to report the same outcome.

I'll tell you about what they did next in a minute, but first I want to cover another extremely important topic and that is the topic of 'habits'.

We will be exploring and utilising the power of habits throughout this journey, especially forming habits, breaking habits and re-forming habits.

Again lots of new understanding has been gained from the study of the brain and the power that habits have over our lives. As I said earlier everything that we have now is a product of who we are, but amazingly who we are is only really a product of our habits and beliefs.

We may think of habits as basic obvious things however, it has now been discovered that habits are embedded deep into our unconscious and are continuously working away to influence who we are and how we behave, without us even being aware.

We now know through studies of people who have experienced damage to parts of their brain that habits are actually locked into an area of the brain called the 'basal ganglia'.

In one particular study, highlighted by Charles Duhigg in his book "The Power of Habit", a man called Eugene Pauly became pivotal in our understanding of the power of habits. Part of Eugene's brain was damaged by a virus such that his short-term memory was non-existent to the extent that he was unable to describe the internal layout of his house when he was sitting in it. And yet when he was hungry or thirsty he would automatically get up go into his kitchen make the drink or food and then come back into the room.

When asked how he would go about making food or drink he was stumped, he couldn't even tell you where his kitchen was, let alone where the food and kettle etc. were kept.

It was discovered that the reason he could automatically get up and make a drink was because he was operating from habit and not memory (remember... he did not have memory!). This was a massive breakthrough in our understanding of habits, because it proved habits are not stored in the same way or in the same place as memory.

Something was driving his behaviour well below his level of consciousness or memory.

Continuing studies of Eugene went on to prove that he was still programming new habits into his brain long after the injury. And we now know how habits are programmed, how they are triggered and how to change them.

This brings me back to the NASA story...

NASA continued to experiment with this phenomenon of the astronauts' brain flipping the image at some point between 21 and 30 days of constant viewing and what they discovered forms the foundation stone of all personal change work today.

They experimented by asking some astronauts to remove their goggles briefly for one day. For example, after 15 days they had one day's break and then continued to wear them again. The results were incredible. Those who took a break still eventually experienced the flipped image, but ONLY AFTER a further 21 – 30 days of wearing the goggles continuously. In other words, the change in neural pathways requires 20 – 30 days of consistent activation. That's how long it takes to create the habit of being able to view an upside down image and see it the right way up.

It is now generally accepted that this applies to ALL habit formation.

This significance of this knowledge is monumental for you and me; it's so empowering because it confirms what many already believed and that is, given who we are is a collection of *beliefs* and *habits,* we now have the ultimate control over who we are going forward.

When it comes to personal transformation we are going to take advantage of this habit process, using it to break old habits and install new habits.

Apart from me, there is another fantastic ally that you will have with you, helping you through this journey and that is your unconscious mind.

There's been a vast amount of research into the unconscious mind, much of it discovered by the great philosophers and scholars of years gone by. However, in today's society with ever-increasing distractions to occupy the attention of our conscious mind, we in the Western world have effectively become disconnected from our unconscious mind in such a way that we are unable to use it to its full potential.

But all is not lost because you STILL have the capability to use your unconscious mind; you simply need to learn how to use it efficiently. With the awareness-raising missions that I will show you in this book you to will be able to harness the power of your unconscious mind to assist you in your personal transformation journey.

Before we move into the meat of this book, I would like to bring to your attention something that will help you move forward: **you must be able to let go of the past!** Now that may sound obvious to you or you may be thinking "Well, I haven't got a past that I need to let go of", but let me assure you, you do.

You see everything that you are right now will become your past when you move forward, when you make the transformations that you need to make in order to achieve the things you want and to be who you want to be. Everything that you have now in some shape or form will be left behind.

One of the biggest challenges people face when trying to transform is breaking the attachment they have to the past. How you are now represents safety and security to your unconscious mind it likes to know what it knows and will try to keep you where you are.

Since you don't want to stay where you are you will have to overcome the pressures your unconscious mind will put on you. But don't worry, I will help you. I will reveal my methods and techniques that will help you spot when this is happening and overcome it.

You see the past is just that - it's a past. It can't be changed. It's fixed. It's gone. What I will be encouraging you to do is to move into the present. The future is unknown, you can plan your future and that's what I'm going to help you do, but exactly how that will be is unknown. What is true is that right now, in this moment, the present is the most wonderful place to be. This is the moment to moment when you have your greatest power, when you can enjoy life to the full, where every moment is to be enjoyed to the full. That's what I'm going to encourage you to do. When you change your mindset to say the past is gone and done, the future is my design, but right now the present is mine to savour, then not only will you succeed with the transformation that you are striving for, but you will also enjoy the rest of your life living in the right now, in the present, in the moment.

I would like to share with you this poem written by Marianne Williamson. For me it sums up the whole essence of what we are all about.

> *Our deepest fear is not that we are inadequate.*
> *Our deepest fear is that we are powerful beyond measure.*
> *It is our light, not our darkness*
> *That most frightens us.*
>
> *We ask ourselves,*
> *Who am I to be brilliant, gorgeous, talented, fabulous?*
> *Actually, who are you NOT to be?*
> *You are a child of God.*
>
> *Your playing small*
> *Does not serve the world.*
> *There's nothing enlightened about shrinking*
> *So that other people won't feel insecure around you.*
>
> *We are all meant to shine,*
> *As children do.*
> *We were born to make manifest*
> *The glory of God that is within us.*
>
> *It's not just in some of us;*
> *It's in everyone.*
>
> *And as we let our own light shine,*
> *We unconsciously give other people permission to do the same.*
> *As we're liberated from our own fear,*
> *Our presence automatically liberates others.*

Now there is something you and I need to do before we can go any further with this book, and that is we need to make a contract.

As I said earlier, these steps are simple, but they are not easy and that means you are at risk of falling prey to at least one of the Seven Deadly Mind Traps™ - the mind trap of *'the path of least resistance'*. Our brain is designed to make life easy for us, to do things in the most efficient way, to keep us on the straight and narrow, which is why if you are serious about making changes and having the life you deserve, I need you to sign a contract.

Now, this contract is partly with me (and I will make some commitments as well), but mainly it is a contract with yourself.

I know there will be events and people that will try to blow you off course. I really don't want them to succeed. I want YOU to succeed, you deserve it. After all, you have already taken one big step by buying this book and reading it to this point - well done!

This contract is an essential part of securing your motivation and resilience and will ensure we get off on the right foot.

So here's the contract - it's pretty simple, but effective.

Many contracts of this nature begin with 'I will' or 'I commit', but you will notice that this one does not. It starts with 'I PROMISE'. This is because we attach much more emotional meaning to a promise, as opposed to a commitment, and I really want you to have enough emotional connection to see you through.

It's easy to break a commitment (remember those New Year's resolutions!), but how do you feel about breaking a promise?

So here we go, I want you to open your journal to a fresh page or take a blank piece of paper and write out these promises exactly as they are listed here:-

1) I PROMISE myself and Peter I will reserve 45minutes per day to read, re-read or digest this book, its bonuses and activities.

2) I PROMISE myself and Peter I will test and try the new behaviours, thoughts and beliefs my mentor Peter gives me.

3) I PROMISE myself and Peter I will suspend any negative disbelief or doubt, so that I can approach new things positively.

# THE Book on Personal Transformation

4) I PROMISE myself and Peter I will choose and maintain an optimistic outlook regardless of what life throws at me.

5) I PROMISE myself and Peter I WILL keep going when things get tough.

SIGNED: ...........................................

DATE: ...............................

I Peter, PROMISE to provide you with the best advice, coaching and mentoring known to me, which is drawn from my study of human behaviour, my passion for knowledge of how the brain works, my modelling of successful people, my own personal experiences and my deep-down desire to help others to have a better, happier, more fulfilling and successful life.

SIGNED:

*Peter Green*

Well done on completing this contract! Excellent! Congratulations!

Reward yourself with a huge pat on the back. You are unique and special. Now... let's get on with your transformational journey.

# CHAPTER 1: What's Lurking in Your Attic? It's Time for a Clear Out.

*"Sometimes you've got to let everything go - purge yourself. If you are unhappy with anything ... whatever is bringing you down, get rid of it. Because you'll find that when you're free, your true creativity, your true self comes out."*

Tina Turner

Before you begin this process, it is essential to have a look at where you are in your life at this moment. You are what you have become.

To become the New You, you will need to travel light, which means leaving behind any excess baggage you have accumulated. There is no shame in having baggage – it is something we all have, it is a part of life. It is what happens to each and every one of us as we travel on life's journey. Many people continue to carry the ever-increasing weight and burden of that baggage around with them for the rest of their lives. But what you are about to discover is the empowering awareness that it doesn't have to be like that.

If you have ever moved house after a long period of living in the same dwelling, you will understand how it feels when you go into your attic for the first time in a long time and start to take stock of what you have accumulated. It can be quite overwhelming at first.

Some items will be sentimental and worth keeping, but as you uncover more and more seemingly-useless items, you begin to ask yourself why on earth did I keep all this junk? It must have seemed like a good idea at the time, but now it's a waste of space and might even end up costing you extra money to have it moved to your new house!

So what do you do?

If you are like most people you would have a thorough clear out, which might involve selling some items at a car boot or yard sale, or you might dispose of them at the local waste disposal centre. This process of de-cluttering can sometimes feel rejuvenating, like lifting a weight from your shoulders as you start afresh in a new home.

Well that's exactly what you need to do with your life – you need to de-clutter to make room for the New You. You are going to have a mental and emotional clear out that will leave you feeling rejuvenated and refreshed, ready for the exciting new journey ahead.

This is an absolutely essential step in the process, it cannot be skipped. If you ignore this part of the process, you will never achieve the New You, you will sabotage every attempt you make.

Now before you start to question whether you really want to become a completely new person, let me make one thing very clear - when I talk about creating the New You through personal transformation, it doesn't mean you will become a completely different person. It doesn't mean there is anything fundamentally wrong with you. It doesn't mean there will be no trace left of the current you, when the process is complete.

Think of it as an upgrade, a refinement, a creation of a newer version of you. You will still be YOU, just a much better version, more successful and happier.

It is important to be honest when working out where you are in life at this point in time. It is human nature to shy away from admitting things are not as good as we would like them to be. However if you are serious about making a transformation, you need to be brutally honest with yourself. No one else will see your answers to this mission (unless you choose to share), so don't hold back. The only person you will be fooling is yourself.

## Mission I:

So… how are we going to do this?

Some 'life balance' questionnaires ask you to look at certain areas of your life and rate them out of 10, but I believe that to be quite a crude method, which is easily influenced by your conscious gatekeeper. I prefer to present you with a series of statements about various aspects of your life and all I want you to do is decide how true they are for you.

For example, if a statement says "I have the perfect job for me" and that is indeed totally true for you, then score that question with a 10, to indicate that it is 100% true. If you feel a statement is mostly true for you, but not totally, then you might decide to score it with an 8, which means it's 80% true for you, and so on.

If you think about the answers for too long, you may be tempted to score them higher than they are in reality, so try to go with your initial 'gut' feeling, don't linger too long. Even though it may feel uncomfortable to give low scores, just go with it, it is best to face it head on now rather than save it up for later.

I want you to stop reading this book now and complete the mission, don't skip over it.

Either put your scores against each question in this book or if you prefer to keep it totally private, open your 'new life' journal to a fresh page (or take a blank piece of paper) and write down the numbers 1 to 10 in a column on the left-hand side of the page to represent each of the questions.

Now, find a quiet place where you will not be disturbed, ensure you are not under any time pressure and rate the following statements as to how they relate to you.

1. I am in the perfect relationship for me

2. I am always true to myself

3. I eat a balanced diet every day

THE Book on Personal Transformation

4. I always feel alert and mentally on the ball

5. I have a fantastic relationship with my parents

6. I am totally clear about my goals, dreams and ambitions

7. I am in full control of my finances

8. I am doing work that I really love

9. I have a high sense of purpose and meaning in my life

10. I imagine the best possible outcomes

11. I have a great support network in my friends

Now if you have not completed the mission, do not turn to the next page. If you are truly serious about this, go back and complete the mission before continuing to read.

Congratulations! If you have turned the page (without cheating) then you must have completed the mission. Well done! You have successfully completed the first step in the process.

So what's the verdict?

I'm sure there may be some ratings on the list that you are uncomfortable with. For many of you it may be the first time you have admitted to yourself that things are far from perfect in certain areas of your life. There's no need to worry, that's exactly why we have done this!

It is important to realise that there is nothing to be gained by directly comparing scores between statements. Some may have far more importance to you than others. For example, you may have rated "I eat a balanced diet every day" with a 5, causing you to raise an eyebrow; but you may have also given a 5 to "I am in the perfect relationship for me", which, assuming you are in a relationship, may cause an uncomfortable twist in your gut.

Again, there is no need to worry - these things need to come to the surface and I will help you move forward. Give yourself a pat on the back for being so honest and read on to find out how it is possible to attend to everything on your list.

You have already identified some of the things you want and need to change, but before embarking upon this journey of change, it's really important that you make peace with who you are now. You need to appreciate all the really great things about you at this point in time.

Now I can already hear that voice in your head saying "There is nothing great about me. Why would I be thinking about changing, if I was already such a great person?" Well I'm here to tell you that you are a great person and just for the moment I need you to thank that inner voice for its input, and suspend your belief that there's nothing great about you, at least until you have completed the next mission.

## Mission II:

Take your journal and open a blank page (or just get a blank piece of paper); on the left-hand side write the heading **"My Achievements"**, and on the right-hand side write the heading **"Things I Admire**

**About Myself"**. Once again find a quiet place where you will not be disturbed and ensure you are not under any time pressure.

You need to write down at least 10 things under each heading. Yes, 10 things! It doesn't matter when in your life you choose to find the information from, but you need to keep going until you have 10 things on each list. If you find it difficult take some time, relax and think back to your childhood and walk through your life from there. You may start to remember many things that you haven't thought about in a while that you are actually very proud of.

Once your lists are complete – 10 things on each side – step back, look at that list and recognise that there are some truly great things about you. You need to acknowledge this, while simultaneously realising that how you are now is not everything about you. You have simply arrived at this point in time via a series of external circumstances and personal choices. By accepting who you are now, you are not letting go of the desire to change, you are merely acknowledging that you are not a bad person.

You already know things are going to change, you have decided it's time to move on, but it is important to realise that you are still a special human being. You need to be at peace with yourself in order to be able to move on to become a newer, fresher version of you.

So many people fail at personal reinvention because they become so obsessed with what they don't like about themselves now and who they have become. This depresses them, their spirit is weakened so much so that they are unable to look forward. "What you focus on is what you get," So if all you focus on is what you don't like about yourself, all you will get is more of that. I don't want this to happen to you, which is why I insist you accept who you are now, turn your head 180° and start to look forwards instead of backwards. Make a promise to yourself that you WILL become a New You.

## Mission III:

Next you are going to create your 'Ditch List'. I want you to take a fresh page in your journal (or use a blank piece of paper) split the page into two columns by drawing a vertical line down the middle and on the left-hand side write the title **"Things I don't want"**. In a moment I'm going to ask you to write down everything you can think of about you and your life that you don't want, and I want you to preface every statement with the phrase **"I don't want…"**

For example "*I don't want to keep arguing with my partner*" or "*I don't want to be angry all the time.*"

Okay let's go! Don't hold back. Think of everything, absolutely everything, you possibly can. If you don't want to write it down the way I described, just keep writing whichever way works for you - it may take a few moments for you to get in the flow.

## Mission IV:

When you have done that, turn to a fresh page or take another sheet of paper and while that's fresh in your mind we are going to find your **WHYWOW™**

I want you to choose a point in the future, maybe 10 or 15 years from now, and write down that date at the top of the page. Now close your eyes and imagine that it is now that date, you are now actually at that point in the future. Imagine you are really there. I want you to imagine that you have <u>not</u> changed any of the things you have just written down, you have remained the same - you put down this book and did not complete any of the missions. What will be happening? How will your life be? Who will be in your life? What will people be saying about you and to you?

I need you to really take yourself there, imagine what it is like in absolute detail - see it, feel it, touch it, smell it, no matter how bad it feels, try to really experience it. I want you to imagine that you are now reflecting and thinking back on the past, and that you had a piece of paper in front of you, as you actually have. Now open your eyes, write on top of the piece of paper **"If only I had…"** and start to write everything that comes into your mind under that heading. All the things you would have done differently to change your future life. Keep writing for at least five minutes. Don't stop, keep the pen moving. If nothing comes to mind immediately, just write gibberish until something comes to mind, if only I had…

You have just created your big **WHY**. This is why you are going to take action, you seriously want to avoid this outcome, move away from it and do everything in your power to stop it becoming your reality. If the above experience evokes a strong negative emotion in you then all the better, the stronger the negative experience, the more these images and feelings will serve as a powerful **WHY** to drive you away from them.

When you've finished, stand-up, walk around a bit, maybe grab a drink of water, and then sit down again.

I now want you to imagine yourself in the future again - same date, same time frame. But this time I want you to imagine that you have taken action on everything you wanted to change at about your life today, and have successfully reinvented yourself. Where are you? What is happening? Who are you with? Whatever your circumstances make it vivid, see it brightly. Again imagine you are actually there. What can you hear? How does it feel? What are your important people saying about you? Savour that experience, make it really bold and bright, joyful and positively exhilarating. An amazing feeling! What success! I knew I could do it! Wooo Hooo!!!

## Mission V:

Next I want you to take another new sheet and write in big letters at the top **"Because I..."**

Now write down everything you can think of that you did from the point you read this book up to where you are now at this point in the future, that wonderful future state. Just keep writing everything that you did, everything that you've changed. What did you do? How did you do it? What changes did you make to get yourself to this point? Keep writing for at least five minutes. Don't stop! Keep the pen moving. If nothing comes to mind, just write gibberish until something comes to mind, Because I...

You have just created what I call your **WOW**, we all need a WOW in order to motivate us to take action and move toward our goals.

Congratulations! By combining both of these lists you have just created you Big **WHYWOW™**

Some things we want to move away from and some we want to move towards. When you add both lists together, the resulting document becomes a very, very powerful motivator to drive you onwards to your ultimate goals.

Now, write a short sentence or two that captures the essence of your **WHYWOW™** and start the sentence with the words **"I am doing this because I want to…"** (Make sure it says something about the **WHY** and the **WOW**). Once you have are happy with what you have written, write it out on a fresh piece of paper using a big, bold marker pen and pin it somewhere where you will see it every day.

Congratulations! You have just changed your brain. You have put in motion a set of reactions in your brain that cannot be reversed. New neural pathways have been created; you've taken the first small step towards creating the New You.

In life everything is created twice, first as a thought and then as reality; you have made the critical first step.

## Mission VI:

Now go back to the list of things you "don't want" and title the right-hand column with **"My Aim Is"** and with all those new thoughts in your mind, with your head turned firmly through 180° and looking forward, write your "180° statements" and ensure you precede every statement with "My aim is …."

For example, if your "I don't want" statement was "I don't want to keep arguing with my partner", then your 180° statement might be "My aim is to understand my partner more, listen to them and improve our relationship."

Now work your way through the list and write a 180° statement for every "I don't want" statement.

At this point, although we are still working on taking stock, we are now going to refine things a little, increase the magnification and zoom in on you.

This is about reinventing you, so we need to take a closer look.

# THE Book on Personal Transformation

Don't worry, all this preliminary work and the related missions will pay off in the end. We need to ensure the New You is created on a strong foundation, there is no point simply creating a weak facade over the top of the old you. Think three little piggies - we need the New You to be built of bricks rather than straw.

Next we are going to perform a characteristics and attitude audit, but first let me share with you why you are like an onion - a very special onion - one that has a diamond at its core.

The diamond is how we are when we are born - bright, fresh, sparkling, full of mystery and potential.

But life grows around us and if we are not careful, forms layer upon layer of false, limiting beliefs, negative thoughts, resentment, anger, low confidence and low self-esteem. But if that does happen, it does not have to stay that way.

NOW is the time to peel back those layers of cynicism, self-doubt and pessimism to reveal the true diamond that is at the heart of you. We are going to polish it, maybe even recut it, but it is still the same diamond, so embrace it and enjoy the ride!

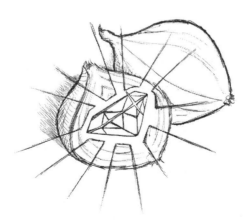

Here we go...

## Mission VII:

Turn to a new page in your journal (or take a blank piece of paper).

This mission takes real honesty and courage. No one knows you better than you, so as your coach I am encouraging you to be honest with yourself, because you deserve that honesty.

As always find a quiet place where you won't be disturbed or overlooked and carry out this mission at a time when you are not time pressured.

Write at the top of the page a heading **"This is me."**

Now, relax, think deeply about yourself and write a list of every word you can possibly think of that in some way describe a characteristic or attitude that you display.

Maybe not all the time, but some times.

I know this will be painful, but I also know that deep down you know all of these things, some of which I'm sure you never have or never will admit to anyone, but you owe it to yourself to admit them to you. So be brave, have courage and write them all down. It does not matter how long this takes, don't rush it. Some people find it easier to think through lots of different situations and scenarios that they have been in and people they have interacted with and then find the words to describe themselves.

Write down everything, good and bad, I am expecting a long list, we humans are complex.

Done! Great! That's excellent work.

Next I want you to go through the list and put a big tick next to all those traits that serve you well and you want to keep going forward as the New You.

Now go through the list again and identify all those that do not serve you well and you will definitely want to 'ditch'. Put a big X next to each one of them.

Now on the right-hand side at the top write **"One thing I could do to help me ditch this is…"**

Now go back through the list again and for each X say to yourself "One thing I could do that would help me ditch this is..." and then write down the first thing that comes into your head, because at a deep level you already know, don't over-analyse.

(Spoiler alert: that little voice will probably pop up again saying things like "You tried that and it didn't work" or "You could never do that, it's not you.") If you experience this or any similar thoughts I suggest you reply in your head by saying something like "Thank you for that input, but that will no longer apply, because it will be the new me not the old one", I'll explain why this works in a later chapter.

Carry on until you have a positive 180° statement for every X on your list.

### Doing, Doing, Done!

### Things to get done before you move on

✓ Treat yourself to a brand spanking new hardback notebook and set it up as your special "My New Life" journal and workbook. This will serve as a great reference point to look back on after your success. It will also really help to keep all your thoughts and notes in one easy accessible place as you go through your transformation journey. Make it your special book. **Check** ☐

✓ Complete the Life-Balance questionnaire with total honesty. Knowing where you really are in all aspects of your life will give you clarity as you make changes. **Check** ☐

✓ Identify your achievements and best qualities, it ensures you start from a sound base; you are already special, in case you forgot. **Check** ☐

✓ Acceptance of who you are now is critical; acceptance will release you to move forward. Complete the mission. **Check** ☐

✓ Create your **WHYWOW**™ statement, write it out and place it where you can see it every day. This will be your essential fuel to propel you forward. **Check** ☐

✓ Generate your 180° statements; get your head facing in the forward direction not backwards. **Check** ☐

✓ REFLECTION: Find a quiet place where you won't be disturbed. Spend at least 20 minutes reflecting on what you did in this chapter. Ask yourself what did I learn from this? **Check** ☐

# CHAPTER 2: Set Sail on Your Voyage of Discovery - Explore, Dream, Discover

*We are all inventors, each sailing out on a voyage of discovery, guided each by a private chart, of which there is no duplicate. The world is all gates, all opportunities.*

Ralph Waldo Emerson

Now we have identified what you don't want, it is time to find out what you really do want.

It's time to discover the real you. What is that diamond really like? Who are you really meant to be?

With your onion peeled back and your diamond shining bright I want you to identify what's really important to you.

Sort your values and define the characteristics that you should have.

I don't want to hear "I can't..." or "because..." as those phrases are signals that there is a limiting belief at work trying to hold you back.

I assure you when you do this next mission deep down there will be a reason why you are drawn to particular choices and that is what we are tapping into, it's already there within you, you just don't know it... yet.

Flick back to the contract; remind yourself what you agreed to do. Suspend disbelief; don't knock it until you have tried it. Remember, trying these missions and going through this process is already part of the New You, so don't let the old you hold you back.

Right, here we go:-

**Mission VIII:**

Turn to a fresh page in your journal, (or take a black piece of paper)

Write across the top in large letters "**I WILL BECOME A PERSON THAT...**"

Now write this sub heading on the left-hand side "**Holds these values**"

I now want you to list as many values as possible that you believe the New You will hold as important.

**Tip:** If you want to take the easy route, skip to **BONUS #1 below.**

Bring out the sheets from the previous missions to help guide and inform you, and remember the visualisation you did of your positive successful future state, remember what values were important to you.

List as many as you can. Here are a few possibilities to get you started:

>   Honesty
>
>   Trustworthiness
>
>   Compassion
>
>   Etc.

Once you have listed them all, select your top five; the five that mean the most to you and are most important to you.

## BONUS #1

If you are finding this difficult go to **www.nowtransform.com** where I have provided a fantastic bonus absolutely free, it's called *The Values Imaginator*™.

It will show you many different values to choose from and includes helpful descriptions to ensure you choose the right ones for you. It even allows you to print off your final selections complete with descriptions.

Just type the website into the address window of the web browser on your computer and away you go.

Done that! Fantastic! You should now be completely clear on your five most important values.

Next we need to work on your characteristics.

I can already hear your inner voice screaming "Hang on a minute Peter, surely, who I am is who I am. I can't change my characteristics."

Again, just for a moment, hold that thought and adopt an open mind.

Remember what we covered earlier... our brains are continually creating new brain cells, and forming new neural pathways and connections through something called neuroplasticity

Why is this so relevant? Well YOU are the sum total of all the neural connections and pathways that have been formed by the experiences and choices you have up to this point in your life. Some of those choices have been conscious and some unconscious, but the resultant connections and pathways are not permanent.

With new thoughts, new experiences and new behaviours your brain will adapt and change with you.

Yes, you are in total control. When you set out to change you, your brain will eventually change with you to become the New You.

Some people call it re-wiring your brain and that is effectively what happens. The missions and methods that I use throughout this book will in time help that process to take place.

It won't happen overnight and sometimes you might wonder if it's happening at all, but eventually you will look back and notice that you have become the New You.

So, on your journal page titled "**I WILL BECOME A PERSON THAT…**" write this sub heading in the middle: "**Has these Characteristics**".

I now want you to list as many characteristics as you can that you believe the New You should have.

You may want to think of some people whom you admire that you aspire to emulate. What characteristics do they have that you value?

**Tip:** If you want to take the easy route, skip to **BONUS #2 below.**

Bring out the sheets from previous missions to help guide and inform you, and remember the visualisation you did of your positive successful future self, remember what characteristics you were displaying, what characteristics got you there.

List as many as you can. Here are a few possibilities to get you started:

>   Courageous
>
>   Determined
>
>   Flexible
>
>   Optimistic
>
>   Etc.

Once you have listed them all, select your top five; the five that are most significant to the success of the New You.

## BONUS #2

If you are finding this difficult, go to **www.nowtransform.com** where I have provided a fantastic bonus absolutely free, it's *The Characteristics Definer*™.

It will show you many different characteristics to choose from and includes helpful descriptions to ensure you get the right ones for you. It even allows you to print off your final selections complete with descriptions.

Just type the website into your computer browser address bar and away you go.

Done that! Fantastic! You should now have your five most significant success characteristics.

So, on your journal page titled "**I WILL BECOME A PERSON THAT…**" write this sub heading on the right-hand side of the page "**Has these attitudes and beliefs**".

All I want you to do here is to think about the attitudes and beliefs that have served you well to get to this New You.

Have a think and try and write down at least five that you think were the most important to you achieving success.

Some examples that people have used in the past are:

"I believe where there is a will there is a way."

"Upbeat and action/solution focused."

"Everyone's view is important, even if it's different to mine."

"I am the master of my own destiny."

"The map is not the territory."

"Respect each other's maps of the world."

"The meaning of your communication is the response you get."

"If it's possible for one person, it's possible for others."

"There is no failure, only feedback."

"Mind and body are part of the same system."

"Every behaviour has a positive intention."

"The person with the most flexibility will control the system."

"If you always do what you've always done, you'll always get what you've always had."

"Your behaviour is not who you are."

"Your perception is your reality."

"You are in charge of your mind, and therefore your results."

"Resistance is a sign of a lack of rapport."

"You cannot not communicate."

"You have all the resources you need to change."

Done that! Fantastic! You should now have your five powerful beliefs/attitudes.

## Purpose

One thing that is extremely valuable for us as humans is to develop a sense of personal purpose.

It gives us a sense of direction, a reason for being and can lead to a sense of fulfilment, all of which contributes to a feeling of happiness and success.

Some people develop this naturally as they go through life and some find it when they experience a traumatic life event, but the majority never even consider it.

Now this may or may not be the first time you have considered this, but either way I want you to start the process of developing a sense of purpose - finding out what you were put on this earth for.

When we find our sense of purpose, it can be both liberating and exhilarating. For some it comes quickly and easily, for others it takes longer, so don't worry if it doesn't happen instantly for you, the important thing is that you start the process.

I remember when I discovered my purpose. It was while I was studying the mind and psychology, when I discovered the fact that **every** human being has all the resources they will ever need, the potential to succeed, to choose to be whoever they want to be inside them.

I realised my mission was to help as many people as possible to understand this, to connect to their inner resources, to achieve success and to enjoy a better life. I find it so sad that millions of people drift through life never realising this and never experiencing the life they could have had.

So what I want you to do is to think back and remember all the occasions in your life when you felt the time just flew by without you noticing. While you're doing this write it down on a fresh page in your journal.

Write down any hobby you have now or have had in the past, a job you enjoyed, any particular tasks in your job you really enjoyed. Spend time on this process, go back to childhood if necessary, and write lots of things down, however insignificant they may seem now, write these down in a list on the left-hand side of your page.

When you have exhausted that list start to think of things that you would love to do, but have never had the chance. Maybe a hobby or just something that you've been drawn to and feel you should have a go at. Continue writing a list.

Now back at the top page on the right-hand side write **"When I do this I feel... Because..."**

Now I want you to go down the list again and complete as many of the **"I feels"** and **"Becauses"** that you can.

Once you have done this, step back and review your list. Have a look for common themes, and note which ones brought out the strongest feelings.

The brain likes to make meaning of things and once set off it will continue in the background. This mission will help direct you to your purpose and your unconscious will work on this continuously, even when you are doing other things. It is possible that while you are doing something mundane, like cleaning the house, the car, or the dishes etc., a thought will suddenly pop into your head relating to this mission. If/when it does quickly write a note on a scrap of paper so you don't forget it.

I'm now going to ask you a series of questions and I want you to write down the first thing that comes into your head for each question, before moving on to the next question.

I recommend you get a piece of card or paper to cover up the next question, only revealing the next one after you have **written your answer to the current one.** I have left space so you can write the answers in the book if you want to.

**Q1** *What will completing this reinvention process bring you?*




**Q2** *When you have* "insert answer to Q1" *what will that bring you?*




**Q3** *When you have* "insert answer to Q2" *what will that bring you?*




**Q4** *When you have* "insert answer to Q3" *what will that bring you?*




...........................

**Keep doing this until you can't go any further.** Each new line will give you an insight into your true underlying reason for wanting to complete this reinvention. When you have your final answer, ensure you write it down - it's part of your big **WHYWOW™**

THE Book on Personal Transformation

### Doing, Doing, Done!
### Things to get done before you move on

✓ Reach inside and uncover your true values. They are there, waiting for you to fully align yourself with them. Strength lies within. **Check** ☐

✓ Define the unique and rich blend of characteristics required by the successful New You. You are not as fixed as you may think; rather flexible enough to be however you choose to be. **Check** ☐

✓ Identify and adopt the most empowering/enlightening beliefs and attitudes that will carry you through. Be mentally strong and healthy for your transformational journey. **Check** ☐

✓ Find your unique purpose. We all have one, somewhere. Once connected with it you will experience true happiness and fulfilment. **Check** ☐

✓ Uncover your bigger WHY. It's a fundamental component of your big WHYWOW™ **Check** ☐

✓ REFLECTION: Find a quiet place where you won't be disturbed. Spend at least 20 minutes reflecting on what you did in this chapter. Ask yourself what did I learn from this? **Check** ☐

# CHAPTER 3: Unleash Your Leonardo Da Vinci and Create Your Masterpiece

*"If we all did the things we are capable of, we would astound ourselves."*

Thomas Edison

Now that you have successfully completed the initial missions, this is where you get really creative. Make sure you are in a place where you can relax and won't be disturbed and get ready to unlock your mind.

You already know all the values, characteristics, attitudes and beliefs of the fresh New You, but what we are really going to work on next is how you are going to be, what you will be doing, what you will not be doing and how you will be doing it.

This is the evolving design of the New You. At the moment it may seem to you to consist of a lot of written lists, but trust me, the process of thinking through them and writing them down is absolutely critical. Something changes in your brain when you write your thoughts down.

## Mission IX:

So here's what I want you to do:

For each of your five core values, characteristics, attitudes/beliefs, I want you to turn to a new page in your journal (or take a blank sheet of paper) and draw three vertical lines to create three columns. Write the 15+ items down the left-hand column. At the top of the middle column, write **"Would be doing"** and at the top of the right-hand column, write **"Would not be doing"**

I now want to focus on behaviours for a moment, and what they really are. For the purpose of this mission I want you to use this definition of a behaviour - "*a behaviour is either something you do or something you say and it's also how you do it and how you say it.*" So when you come to describe behaviours I want you to check that how you are describing them fits that definition.

Taking each item in turn you need to work down the list identifying the behaviours that a person would do and definitely not do for each of the items. You may find it helpful to use the descriptions from the bonus items as a guide.

For example:

Let's say you choose the characteristic "courageous" - you might be tempted under the "Would be doing" column to write something like "Really goes for it", but this does not fit the description of behaviours that I mentioned above. It could be re-written as "Steps up and carries out tasks even when they seem daunting." Under the "Would not be doing" column you would then write "Sits back and avoids tasks that are considered to be daunting."

Now that you have completed the first stage of the mission, we are going to move away from doing and start to think about being. You see, deep down we are human beings and not human doings.

How we perceive ourselves is critical to how we behave, so my question now is "How are you going to be?"

Using your 15+ items as a guide, you are going to craft your **"I am…"** statement.

An example would be: "I am a confident and considerate person, who focuses on their goals and achieves success, while taking the time to support and involve others."

The reason it is important to have an **"I am…"** statement is because of what I call the **BE-DO-HAVE** principle.

When you choose to **BE** a certain way, you will automatically **DO** things the right way, which will result in you **HAVING** the things that you want in your life.

Spend some time now and craft your own statement, ensure it is powerful and really captures the essence of the New You.

Most people approach this belief the wrong way. They simply focus on what they want to have, don't get the results they want and give up feeling like a failure. But not you - you now know the better way.

The key to all of this change work is mind over matter. It's the matter of brain not brawn that makes the difference.

Firstly, you really have to believe that you CAN be like this. There goes that inner voice again, "Yes, but....." and if that's what's happening in your head right now, just thank it for its contribution and then let that thought go.

Just say to yourself (say it out loud if it's safe to do so):

I am a *confident and considerate person etc...* (Substitute the words that are right for you)

This is an affirmation, something I want you to say to yourself on a regular basis. Remember to keep it in the current tense (I am) as if it has already happened. (I'll explain more about why you should do this later in this chapter)

**PRSF™**

**Personal Reinvention Success Formula:**

**BELIEFS create THOUGHTS create FEELINGS create BEHAVIOURS create RESULTS.**

Keep this formula in mind; it is your secret to success. Just ask any athlete or successful entrepreneur (as I have done many times) and they will agree or have their own similar version.

As Henry Ford famously said: "*If you think you can or you think you can't, you're usually right.*"

So we have dealt with the 'beliefs' part of the success formula, now let's move on to the 'thoughts' section.

# Visualisation

I'm now going to give you the tool that many successful people use. The most common term for this tool is visualisation and it works a treat for the thoughts section of the success formula. Have a go as per my instructions, but feel free to make it yours - tweak it a bit if you want, but ensure you keep the essence intact.

The best time to do this is just as you are going to sleep at night or just when you are waking in the morning. This is because at these times the gatekeeper to your unconscious is not fully awake and you can program things into your unconscious more easily. You can of course also do this at any time of day when you have some quiet time.

Firstly, find somewhere quiet where you will not be disturbed. Sit down in a chair with your back upright and the underside of your forearms resting either on your legs or on the arms of the chair.

Choose a behaviour that you want to work on and the situation where you want to use it.

Now, close your eyes and take a few deep breaths, breathing in through your mouth and out through your nose. Focus on how the air exits your nose. Notice how it feels, notice the complexity of the sounds that it makes. Do this for a few minutes and relax your whole body, starting from the top of your head and working all the way down to the tips of your toes.

Imagine yourself in the situation that you have chosen to focus on. See yourself. Step into yourself. Be there in that situation. Now feel yourself behaving the way that you would want to behave. Notice how it feels to be like that. Play out the positive scenario that you envisage. Pay attention to what you're saying notice. Recognise how you are behaving. Play out various 'what if' versions of the same scenario, each time behaving the way that you choose. Notice how it feels, what you say and how you said it.

If you have time, switch to a different characteristic, behaviour and scenario, and do the same thing again. All the time believe and experience it as if it is real. Stop when ready, open your eyes and slowly bring yourself back into the present.

Stop reading and have a go now, you might want to record yourself speaking the three paragraphs and then play it back so you can close your eyes and follow the mission more easily. Feel free to embellish it, make it longer and more thorough, personalised for you. I'm sure you get the gist of it.

How was that?

Well, even if you found that empowering and enjoyable you will not appreciate the awesome power of its true affect until you are in that imagined situation for real.

Let me explain a little about what you just did. There are two things to be aware of. Firstly, the brain cannot really tell the difference between imagined events and real events, because they are both ultimately presented to the brain through the same information systems. And secondly, I am sure you are familiar with the fact that the more you practice something, the more familiar it becomes and the easier it becomes to do - this process is called 'Mental Rehearsal'.

Many people have used this technique. Jack Nicklaus, the famous golfer, was a regular user of this process and attributed it as a major contribution to his success.

Before a big match he would visualise himself playing every single hole, practising different ways of playing it, noticing in his mind which ones worked best. He would even visualise himself hitting into a poor position in the trees and then visualise how he would play the best shot out of that bad situation. If he did then find himself in that bad position, he 'felt' he had already been there once and immediately felt confident that he knew how best to play out of it. Guess what? On the majority of occasions, that's exactly what he did!

Consider this part of the process as you begin **setting yourself up for success,** programming your brain for the new successful you.

## Stephen's Story

Stephen lived in Coventry and his life was a mess. He was divorced and had a son he had not seen for ten years. His council flat resembled a rubbish dump. School had not engaged him and he had left with few qualifications. His jobs had been menial and manual, mostly self-employed. His circle of friends regularly spent their time and money drinking and gambling in the pub.

It was Christmas and he was drunk again. He'd just had a blazing row with his family. He wasn't sure whether it was because they wouldn't let him drive home drunk or because he had just revealed to them that he was hooked on cocaine!

Stephen decided it was time for change! And so began his change process.

Although not academic, he had discovered that he was a quick learner, who was pretty good at reading and dealing with people.

Over the next few years, an amazing transformation took place. He got himself a real job and discovered that people thought he was good at it. He found he didn't need academic ability, just common sense (street nouse), the ability to read people and resilience; he had all of these qualities in abundance.

His self-confidence grew; he moved jobs several times, each time increasing his salary. He eventually arrived at a level that he had previously believed was only for 'clever' people, not for the likes of him!

He found a new partner through online dating and decided to give his flat a complete makeover. In the process of that he discovered he was also pretty good at DIY.

If Stephen's 'old self' could have gone forward in time, he would not have even begun to recognise himself now.

## Doing, Doing, Done!

### Things to get done before you move on

- ✓ Uncover the characteristics of the New You. It's important to know what the New You would be doing and would not be doing. **Check** ☐

- ✓ Craft your "I am" statement. Take your time, refine it, make sure it really resonates with you and defines the New You. **Check** ☐

- ✓ Establish your Be-Do-Have. Knowing how to be drives what you do, which creates what you have. **Check** ☐

- ✓ Embrace the personal reinvention success formula, (PRSF™). Your Beliefs create your Thoughts, which create your Feelings, which create your Behaviours, which create your Results. Align all these and you will succeed. **Check** ☐

- ✓ Everything is created twice. Master the process of true 'Mental Rehearsal'. This will give you the best possible chance of getting it right and boost your confidence. **Check** ☐

- ✓ REFLECTION: Find a quiet place where you won't be disturbed. Spend at least 20 minutes reflecting on what you did in this chapter. Ask yourself what did I learn from this? **Check** ☐

# CHAPTER 4: Let the Butterfly Emerge - Time to Act Like You Belong

*"The way to develop self-confidence is to do the thing you fear and get a record of successful experiences behind you. Destiny is not a matter of chance, it is a matter of choice; it is not a thing to be waited for, it is a thing to be achieved."*

William Jennings Bryan

This is it! Preparation time is now over - it's time to put your masterpiece into action.

There is no easy way to start and there is no time like now.

You may be tempted to seek permission, to find someone who you can tell your plans to, but I advise against this. If the person is close to you they may be overprotective and try to talk you out of it. They will think this will help to protect you, but it will only hold you back. If the person is not close to you they may choose to ridicule you or sabotage your plans. If you really need to confide in someone, carefully sound out a trusted colleague/friend, explain your situations and the reasons for change and explain to them how they can best help you. Explain what you **do** want from them and explain what you **don't** want from them; ensure they genuinely understand this before you go into more detail.

Initially it's best not to start with something too major or radical. Remember this is a journey, not a sprint. Start with small, incremental steps and consider that a journey of 1000 miles always starts with the first couple of steps.

But start you must. You can't wait for the right moment - I can assure you it will never arrive, no matter how long you procrastinate. The right moment is already here.

Remember you don't have to ask anyone's permission to try this; the only person you are accountable to is you.

There is no doubt that you will experience 'Fantasy Experienced As Real' (or FEAR as it's commonly known), it's only natural, but the important thing is not to let it paralyse you.

It's all about attitude and acting. I want you to **act as if you belong**. You will have already visualised most of this, so it won't be the first time you experience it, and if you haven't mentally rehearsed it then make sure you do before you go forward.

Let's consider attitude for a moment. Let's say you are about to go out and you want to be more upbeat about things, rather than always focusing on the negative. Ask yourself what attitude would someone who is upbeat about things have? How would they look? How would they feel? How would they behave? Armed with this information, practice this behaviour for real. There is no easy way to get this started - as Susan Jeffers said, "*Just feel the fear and do it anyway.*"

We have already discussed how practice makes perfect, but initially it may feel awkward, wrong, and difficult. Trust me; it will eventually become second nature.

The power of habits is your greatest ally; this power will be working in your favour all the time. The human brain is amazing. It can learn anything and eventually do it without thinking. This process of learning and assimilation is called the **'competence consciousness sequence'** and it goes through four phases.

It begins with **'unconscious-incompetence'.** This is the phase where we just don't know how poorly we can do something. For example, we would like to drive a car, but we are too young to try, therefore we do not know our level of incompetence, therefore the belief is unconscious.

The next phase is **'conscious-incompetence'**. This is when we become aware of just how much we don't know how to do something. For example, the first driving lesson. I remember mine, do you remember yours? It felt like there was so much to remember, too much to ever be able to master. At this point we're now conscious of our level of incompetence.

The next phase is **'conscious-competence'**. This is when we have mastered how to do it, but it takes a lot of conscious effort and attention to do so. For example, when you have completed a number of driving lessons and your instructor says you're ready for your test. It means you can do the task, but you still have to pay attention to it at a conscious level.

And the final phase is **'unconscious-competence'**. This is when you seem to be able to do it well, without really thinking about it. For example, when you've been driving for a while and you reach your destination and realise that you can't remember getting there. Your mind was on other things, but somehow you seem to have safely negotiated all the junctions and hazards. This is because the repetition of the behaviour of driving has now been burnt into your unconscious mind and your unconscious mind is more than capable of taking care of it for you.

This is exactly what you're going to do with the behaviours associated with the New You. You will keep doing them until one day you will look back and say "This is me now, it feels so natural. I don't recognise that old version of me. When did the change happen?"

## Your Greatest Ally is Your Greatest Threat

So that's the process, but what about the mindset you will require while doing this. Well not surprisingly it needs to be a tough one, as there will be many challenges along the way waiting to throw you off course.

The first thing to consider is what happens when things don't go to according to plan or as some people like to call it - failure. To deal with this there is a very important belief that I would like you to adopt.

"*Act like you belong in that persona and body, and wait for the feelings to catch up.*"

"Ooooh", I hear your inner voice saying, "But if I'm acting, I'm only pretending and that's not going to help".

Well, it will help, let me explain why. When an actor is to play a role he studies everything about the character and uses a method to become that person so convincingly that we believe it is real. When he's finished the play/movie, he will become himself again, he is only pretending to try to convince the audience. But while he is playing that character, he truly believes he is that character. (In fact some actors actually have trouble going in and out of character and will choose to stay in character for the entire day of filming, even when they are off set).

You can use exactly the same approach, only you are not pretending and there is only one audience member you are trying to convince and that is your unconscious.

Your unconscious is totally subservient to your beliefs. It does not have the ability to have any view or opinion (it is your conscious mind that does that). After consistently experiencing you behaving differently for a period of time, your unconscious will believe that that is who you are. It will then reorganise all your internal resources to support that.

In other words, at some point in the future, you won't even have to think consciously about being the New You, you will just be like that, because that will be you. Your unconscious will believe that's you and all your behaviours will align with that automatically, and that's why I say your unconscious is your greatest ally.

But, as I mentioned previously, although your unconscious mind is your greatest ally, it can also seem to be your greatest challenge. How can this be?

Well, as I have said before, your unconscious has one purpose in life, which is to serve you, to protect you, to make sure that you stay as you. In order to do this it has set up a number of reference points that represent what it knows to be the normal you. Some people refer to this as a comfort zone, because its purpose is to maintain you and keep you comfortable. If it detects that you are drifting off course or are doing things that are not aligned with what it knows to be the normal you, it will take action to alert you and to get you back on course.

It has two main ways of protecting you. Firstly over thousands of years it has evolved a method to protect you from danger, which is how we survived and how we evolved as a species. If danger was detected, such as a sabre-toothed tiger approaching from the bushes, then this detection triggered an automatic response mechanism. Your brain instantly released a cocktail of potent chemicals designed to keep you alive. One of the major chemicals released was adrenaline, which was to prepare you for one of two actions: either run away or stand and fight (often referred to as the fight or flight mechanism). It worked! These chemicals increased your heart rate, constricted your blood vessels, and diverted blood from brain to muscles. You will probably recognise how this feels: a racing heart, sweaty palms, knotted stomach, and unfocused mind. Yes you recognise those feelings don't you? Often referred to as Fantasy Experienced As Real or FEAR.

The fight or flight response has been extremely useful, it has kept us alive and allowed us to evolve. We need it even today - just replace the sabre-toothed tiger with a large truck speeding towards you as you step off the path/sidewalk to cross the road. You'll be glad you somehow leapt back to safety in a flash without even thinking about it - thanks to your unconscious mind.

The trouble comes with the addition of our more advanced conscious brain, which has the capability to imagine in vivid details absolutely anything we choose to think of. For example, you are getting ready to go out and have decided that you are going to behave differently. Maybe you're going to smile more often, dress slightly different, or engage with people more positively. Your imagination kicks into action and imagines everything going wrong; people laughing at you or bumping into a colleague who teases you. These are not really threatening events, but you associate bad feelings with those thoughts, they become a threat of sorts and immediately the fight or flight response kicks in, (because it's become automatic over millions of years), the chemicals spill out into your blood stream and you start to get all those feelings of nervousness and fear. So much so that you decide not to go out at all, and all this has taken place in the space of a few seconds, and it is all imagined.

The key to success is to control your thoughts. As powerful as they seem they are in your control, IF you choose to control them. Here's what you can do. As soon as you realise what is happening to you, you can choose to look at the situation differently. Firstly thank your unconscious for trying to keep you safe and then say something like "I am in control, I am safe. This is the new me I choose to be and no harm will come to me, in fact only good." "If some people are unsure it is just because they are afraid of change, they are welcome to their thoughts. Their thoughts and their words cannot hurt me." That will help to reduce the concept of threat/danger and reduce the chemical release. You can also burn some energy, maybe by taking a short brisk walk, as this will help to burn off the chemicals that have already been released and hence reduce the symptoms.

The second way that your unconscious protects you is through a lower level system, also designed to keep you safe and in your comfort zone and this is called the 'Psycho-Cybernetic Mechanism'. We will call it your PCM.

This is the system that keeps an eye on how you are **being**. It has a reference point of what and how 'you' are, based on what it has derived over the years you've been alive.

It's a bit like the thermostat on your heating system. The temperature you set is the reference point. If the system detects that the room is cooler or hotter than the reference point it will increase or decrease the heating accordingly.

If you're PCM detects that you have moved away from your reference point, it will slowly guide you back. So let's say you choose to act differently; you overcome the initial fears and you try it. Things go okay; no disasters (despite what your imagination tried to con you into believing), but it felt very uncomfortable and strange, and it felt like it wasn't really you. Those uncomfortable feelings are being created by your PCM to try and coax you back to what it believes is the normal you.

If these feelings are left unchecked you would soon find yourself right back where you started.

The key to overcoming this low-level protection process is to acknowledge the feelings, thank your PCM for trying to help and then change the way you interpret the feelings. Choose to look at those feelings as a positive sign, a sign that you are definitely moving in the right direction. Treat them as small signs of success. Feelings contain energy; use the energy as positive reward to keep you going.

After a period of time, maybe only days or weeks, you will suddenly notice that you don't have these feelings anymore. You probably won't remember when they stopped, but what it means is that you have now reset your PCM reference point; you are becoming the New You.

## Boosting Your Self Belief

You will no doubt get unsolicited feedback from a range of people and there is only one person whose feedback you should trust, and that is YOU.

You know exactly what you are trying to achieve and why. Become self-reliant on your feedback and remember this when things don't go as planned - *"failure only occurs when you give up trying, everything else is just feedback."* Thomas Edison reportedly tried 9999 attempts to create the filament of the electric light bulb before he found the one that worked. When asked about how he coped with all those failures, he reportedly replied that he had just discovered 9999 compounds that were not suitable! He didn't see them as failures.

So if you try something and it doesn't go the way you want it to, refine it and try again.

One the most powerful things you can do to help yourself during this phase is to boost your self-belief. In fact I want you to get to the point of TSB, that's Total Self-Belief.

But what is self-belief and how can you get it or increase it?

It's a mix of a few different things. It's a feeling of being good enough and it's about having a healthy appreciation of yourself. It's a belief that you are much bigger than anything life may throw at you, accompanied by a belief that "where there is a will there is a way."

Some of the characteristics that support self-belief are:

> Optimism
>
> Bravado
>
> Energy
>
> Temerity
>
> Audacity
>
> Self-Assurance

The best way to work on your self-belief is on two fronts.

Firstly work on your belief about yourself. There is a reason why this is so important, not just for self-belief and confidence, but also for any other aspect of yourself.

You remember how your unconscious has one purpose and that is to serve you? Well one way it does this is to ensure that your beliefs are proven. What do I mean by this?

It's called "***What the thinker thinks, the prover proves.***"

It is well-established that we don't notice everything that we see or hear. Our brain would be totally overloaded with the 1.2 million bits of information per second that bombard our senses, so the brain has developed a screening and filtering system.

One of the key programs for the filters is your beliefs. We feel reassured when we notice that our beliefs are true. But of course a belief is only a belief. Just because we believe it is true does not actually make it true. The more we see evidence that supports it, the more comfortable we feel. So the filters will let through evidence that proves our beliefs and block or delete anything that might disprove them.

Let's use an example around a belief about yourself. Imagine you believe you are really useless presenter. On one of the few occasions you were persuaded to make a presentation, you noticed your hands were shaking, you got some of your words mixed up and you turned bright red. Inside a little voice says, "See, I knew I was a useless presenter" (*what the thinker thinks, the prover proves*). But what also happened that you didn't notice was, the audience enjoyed what you had to say, they didn't notice your hands shaking, they forgave your small mix up because they know what it's like presenting at short notice and thought you did better than they could have done, and your voice was clear and audible. All of those things were true, but you only noticed the things that supported your belief.

It is important to hold positive beliefs about yourself as they will become reinforced. If you hold negative beliefs about yourself they will also become reinforced.

Sometimes you will receive criticism that is intended to hurt or destabilise you. Unfortunately it's the nature of the world we live in, you can't change the people, but you can change yourself and how you deal with and interpret things. So I am going to ask you to identify and adopt some useful beliefs about yourself

What three key beliefs, if you totally believe them to be true, would make the most significant difference to your life?

Write them down and then choose to adopt these beliefs, suspend the voice that says "Yeah, but they are not true", and say, "I don't know that yet, I'm going to adopt and act as if these beliefs are true."

Some people refer to this as "faking it" or "fake it 'til you make it". I don't like either of those phrases because I believe they have negative connotations - fake is generally a bad thing. I much prefer to say **"act as if you belong"** i.e. belong in the new persona you are creating.

When you do receive strong criticism, the first thing to do is not overreact, then step back and make sure you have heard correctly. If it is something you have done and you know it was wrong, then don't cover up; take a deep breath, apologise, decide what you would do next time and move on.

If you have not done anything wrong you may need to assert your right to have an opinion and your right to be who you are. Assert means you do that without emotion or anger, but with a self-assured "matter-of-fact-ness", while still acknowledging the other person's right to have a view.

The important thing is not to let it 'infect' your self-belief. If it does you will begin to be plagued with self-doubt instead of empowered with self-belief.

So that's some of the internal stuff, now what about externally?

Next I'm going to ask you to be cheerful. No doubt you may say *"I've got nothing to be cheerful about. How do expect me to be cheerful?"* Well, firstly there have been numerous scientific studies conducted, which prove that being cheerful and smiling actually changes the chemical balance in the brain. More endorphins are released when we smile - endorphins are the chemicals that make us feel good, happy and contented. Also, you are much more likely to be received well by others; they will seem to treat you differently if you are happy and cheerful.

There is a part of our brain, called the limbic system, which is connected to our emotions. The limbic system is known as an open loop system, unlike the PCM which is closed loop. The open loop system means that it can be influenced externally. This is why we tend to feel other people's emotions; it's why we might shed a tear after watching a sad film. It is also why we tend to laugh when other people laugh, and smile back when someone smiles at us. It's an automatic response. So if you choose to smile more often, you are likely to receive more positive smiles and responses back from others.

That's the science behind why it's worth being more cheerful, now let's address the issue of "I can't because I have nothing to be cheerful about."

It comes back to the fact that only you are in ultimate control of how you feel, not your circumstances. In other words you can literally

**choose** to be more cheerful, **choose** not to look backwards. As weird as this may sound, it is totally true, so go out there and choose to be more cheerful, practice a smile and notice the difference on the inside and the outside.

It's also been shown that people with a positive disposition are generally healthier and live longer. And before you mention it, there is very little influence from a genetic perspective; most of our demeanour is learned. The author Martin Seligman even wrote a book about it called "Learned Optimism."

Here's a caveat: It's worth pointing out here that I am not advocating you ignore serious emotions and go around with an annoying "happy clappy everything is wonderful" mentality. It's important to experience a range of emotions - it's okay to be sad and cry occasionally, after all it's what makes us human. All I am suggesting is that you choose when to be sad or happy and not allow yourself to be controlled by others or by circumstances.

When first starting out to be the New You, I suggest you go to somewhere totally new, a place where you are sure you will not bump into anyone you know - maybe a large shopping centre, where you can still have an opportunity to interact with people, stallholders, shop assistants, and fellow shoppers. Go out with the intention to fully immerse yourself in the New You, to really get to know what it feels like. No one will judge you because as far as they are concerned, this is you and you have always been like that. This is a great way to get the early jitters out of the way and before you know it you will be like this all the time.

## Reclaim Your Warrior Spirit

There is no doubt that you are going to need to muster up some courage. Your mind will play havoc with your thinking and your friends and family may be challenging and somewhat hurtful, but all with the best of intentions. You will have to psyche yourself up for this and prepare your responses.

I call this reclaiming your 'warrior spirit'. Deep down in all of us there are the remnants of a warrior, a desire to stand up and fight for what is ours. History is littered with examples of ordinary men and women carrying out heroic and courageous acts when standing up for what they really believe is right, or protecting the honour of someone close, or fighting for what is rightfully theirs.

It is why we all love the films where the underdog suddenly rears up and asserts his or herself and ultimately wins the day. We relate to that spirit within us all and we can call upon it in times of need. This is what I have in mind for you (minus any anger and violence of course). You are a free spirit, you have the right to make this choice, you have the right to be whoever you want to be, no one owns you, and no one controls you. This is your future, your destiny, which is at stake.

Not everyone will understand or like what you are doing, but you are not here to please everyone. Show that spirit, prime yourself for the fight, rise up and claim your right to be you. Put on your armour, load up your language skills and step out into the new dawn - reclaim your warrior spirit.

Important caveat: I am always working on the assumption that the New You is ecologically and socially balanced. By that I mean that no one is going to be harmed or seriously disadvantaged by any of your plans. For example, if the New You intends to leave your family to restart anew, you must weigh up the pros and cons, taking into account how people will be affected and making suitable provisions to ensure that everyone is looked after.

## The Critical Conversations with Yourself!

I want to speak about self-talk. I am aware that some people don't like to admit they have self-talk, believing that some might consider them to be unbalanced or mentally unwell. So firstly let me explain that there is a huge difference between hearing voices in your head that tell you to do evil things and the on-going chatter that we all have within ourselves, often in our own voice. We all have it, it's a natural human thing and we refer to it as self-talk. I'm sure you have heard the phrase 'your mind's eye', well this is 'your mind's voice or voices'.

So having established what it is, what do we know about it?

Self-talk comes in two main forms. Firstly there is the **inner critic** (this will spring into action either before, during or after something happens) and secondly there is the **inner supporter.**

Very often you will find that the most dominant voice is the inner critic. This is mainly due to the fact that you've received much more negative or critical feedback, as opposed to supportive or positive feedback, through your life up to this point. In fact it is estimated that the average person in the world now has been told they "can't" about 60,000 times by the time they are 18 - no wonder the inner critic feels strong, it's been well fed!

So, what might you hear and say?

The first thing to establish is that you can take some control of your self-talk. The biggest problem is that the inner critic will eventually influence your unconscious if it is allowed to continually put you down.

Let's examine how this works. Imagine you have just made an error, maybe dropped something, deleted an important file or sent a sensitive e-mail to the wrong person. Assuming there are no other people around, most of us would curse under our breath or in our heads and say things like "You stupid idiot!", "You useless berk!" or in some cases much, much worse!

Here's the problem, if your unconscious continually hears "You're stupid", "You're an idiot", "You're useless", it will work on that information. As we've mentioned before it makes no judgement, but if stupid and useless are what it believes you are, because it's heard it so many times, then that's what it will ensure you are.

But it's not all doom and gloom - the same goes for positive encouragement. The more positive and encouraging things your unconscious hears, the more it believes. So what can you do?

The first step is to become aware of which voice is more dominant for you. Notice every time you recognise the critic saying something and when you do, start to answer it back with a polite correction.

For example, let's say you are trying to be the New You and you say something that does not come out as you intended. You might notice that the critic says "See, I told you it would never work, it's a disaster". If this happens, answer back in your head with the supporter, saying something like this "Thank you for that, it's not a disaster, I'm still practising and I'm doing very well. I'm totally capable of mastering this" and/or "I am a confident and outgoing person".

If you do something like that every time you catch yourself putting yourself down, you will gradually retrain the critic to be quieter and your supporter to be more prominent, the net effect being that your unconscious will understand you to be a confident and outgoing person and over time will automatically adjust your behaviours to be in line with that view.

A useful phrase to remember is this: "*Put the behaviours into action and the feelings will join you.*" In other words, it may feel uncomfortable at the moment, but eventually it will just feel normal.

Try this as a little experiment: If you wear a watch, remove it now and put it on the other wrist. Most of us tend to have a preference for which wrist we wear our watch on. Having done that notice how it feels. You are most likely experiencing a feeling of uncomfortable, feels odd, not normal. That's your unconscious, and it will keep nudging you that something is not quite right. Some people feel a stronger feeling of "Oh no, this is just wrong. I can't wear it on that wrist".

Regardless of the uncomfortable feelings, I want you to persevere and keep it on that new wrist for another 24 hours. I guarantee that sometime tomorrow you will have forgotten that is on the other wrist and if you left it there for a week or so, it would just feel normal.

It's the same with the New You, initially it will feel uncomfortable and not normal. Persevere, manage your self-talk and in time it will just be the normal you.

## BONUS #3

Free audio download of my interview with David Hyner.

David's story of his own personal reinvention will inspire you, as it has me and countless others. He shares how he went from stressed-out chef to successful and sought-after international speaker.

I am making this awesome interview available to you totally free as a Thank You for buying my book. Just go the website **www.nowtransform.com** and click on the **Bonus #3** link to listen or download the MP3.

## Doing, Doing, Done!
## Things to get done before you move on

- ✓ There is no easy way to start, just "Act like you belong" in that new persona and wait for the feelings to catch up. **Check** ☐

- ✓ Trust and reply upon the Competence Conscious Sequence. It's served you well up to now and will help you achieve your goals here. **Check** ☐

- ✓ Tame your natural Flight or Fight responses. They keep you alive and help you enjoy excitement. It's only adrenaline, make friends with it. **Check** ☐

- ✓ Get in touch with your PCM. Recognise when it's operating and reprogram it to be comfortable with the New You. **Check** ☐

- ✓ Believe in Yourself. Work on building up to TSB - Total Self Belief - it will hold you strong at your core during any turbulence! **Check** ☐

- ✓ Feed your 'Prover' - the most useful information to reinforce the New You. **Check** ☐

- ✓ Choose to be cheerful. It will serve you and others well. Don't under estimate its power. **Check** ☐

- ✓ Reconnect with your 'Warrior Spirit', it's somewhere within all of us. **Check** ☐

- ✓ Take control of those Crucial Conversations that you have with yourself. They will make or break your success. **Check** ☐

- ✓ REFLECTION: Find a quiet place where you won't be disturbed. Spend at least 20 minutes reflecting on what you did in this chapter. Ask yourself what did I learn from this? **Check** ☐

# CHAPTER 5: Roll Call! Identify the Sappers and the Zappers

*"Be careful the environment you choose for it will shape you; be careful the friends you choose for you will become like them."*

W Clement Stone

You should now be progressing well working on the New You. You may have noticed everything we have done so far has been working from the inside out, and we have been doing that for a reason. Quite simply, it does not work the other way round. If you attempt this process from the outside in, it would be similar to wearing a mask and at some point the mask would slip off and you would be right back where you started.

But now it is time to look outwards, to take a look at who is around you and who you spend your time with.

There is a very important reason why you need to consider this aspect of your situation; it will play a crucial role in how successful your change will be.

You see, many studies have shown that we become aligned with those we spend most time with, aligned with their beliefs and life aspirations.

As tough and dramatic as this may sound, if those beliefs aspirations are not aligned with the New You, then you must consider changing your circle.

Not all of your current circle will understand what you are doing or why you are doing it. Inevitably they will try to convince you that what you are doing is wrong and they may even try to talk you out of it.

It will be very difficult to maintain your enthusiasm, drive and warrior spirit under those conditions.

Also, if we assume you don't change your circle and you don't manage to fight your way through the nay-sayers and complete your transformation into the New You, how well will you now fit in with the current crowd? You may find that you have little in common with them anymore.

My advice is to undertake this process of changing your circle as a gradual evolution rather than one big bang. Think about where you might meet people who will be more aligned with the New You, go out and mingle, make a few new friends without disconnecting completely from your current crowd. Slowly you will migrate towards those who are aligned with the New You. Some of your current crowd may well migrate with you, you never know, they may also want to change. In time you will find your new crowd. You will find that those who don't come with you will slowly drift off of their own accord, particularly as you will be seeing them less frequently.

However, in some circumstances you may have to burn some bridges, it's the only way. In fact if you don't burn some bridges it will be all too easy to slip back to how you were - your brain will always take the path of least resistance. The answer is to make sure that some of these paths are blocked, i.e. no return is possible.

## Sappers and Zappers

At some point in this process you will need to make an assessment of the people around you. I call this identifying your Sappers and Zappers.

**Sappers:** These are the people who seem to sap your energy, enthusiasm and strength. A colleague of mine calls them "mood vampires".

These are the people who will always tell you "It will never work", "This is not really you, you'll get hurt", spreading doom and gloom. Some will have your best interests at heart (from their perspective), others will be doing it purely because that's the pessimistic, cynical kind of person they have become.

Whenever you come into contact with them they sap your energy and leave you with a darkened mood. After spending time with them you feel low.

**Zappers:** These are people who inject energy and enthusiasm, like a zap of energy from a lightning bolt, they provide encouragement. They listen with the intent to understand you and then support you. They provide genuine and valuable feedback and they are generally optimistic.

When you leave their company you feel uplifted, refreshed and full of energy and excitement about the possibilities that lie ahead.

So make a decision, who do you want in your team? Who do you want in your support network?

Enlist the Zappers and ditch the Sappers.

As I mentioned earlier, some of the sappers may disconnect from you of their own choice, but some you will have to make the conscious choice to say goodbye to.

## Ditch, Keep or Sound Out

Now it's time to take out your journal again. Turn to a fresh page (or take a blank piece of paper).

Make a list of everyone that you currently come into contact with.

Next, go down that list and write against each one either a D, a K or an S.

For anyone that you feel certain fits into the category of a Sapper, mark with a D for Ditch.

For anyone you feel will definitely support you, mark with a K for Keep.

For anyone you are not really sure about, mark with an S for Sound Out.

With anyone you have marked with an S, you will need to have a conversation to test the water and get a feel for how they might react to the New You.

For those you marked with a D, make some time to see them or note a point when you know you will have some time with them. How you do the 'ditching' is really up to you and will be influenced by the type of relationship you have with them, but I suggest when the time is right, you have an adult to adult conversation with them, to explain that you are moving on to pastures new. Don't make it personal; it's your choice and it's time for a change. Some of them may not understand and protest, but on the other hand be prepared for your assessment to be wrong, some of them may well turn out to be supporters. Alternatively, you could wait and see if they drift away of their own accord.

Remember, your past is just that. It's in the past and you will need to come to terms with letting go of your past, in order to fully embrace your future.

Commitment to your change is key - answer the following question:

On a scale of 1 to 10, how likely are you to see this change through to the end?

Where 1 is not very likely, just toying with the idea and 10 is absolutely determined, nothing will deter me from achieving my goal of the new me.

Make sure you have that number in your head before you turn the page...

THE Book on Personal Transformation

If you scored 8 or less I want you to answer the following questions.

What would need to change for you to score a 10?

What could you do differently that would allow you to score 10?

What would need to be different for you to score 10?

What is holding you back?

I know you know, deep down you know the answer, that's why you did not say 10.

Your most important next job is to be honest with yourself, identify the reasons and go out and fix them. Whatever it takes you must resolve them; otherwise you will seriously reduce your chance of success.

This is a question I ask my coaching clients. I don't let them move on until we have clearly identified the blocks and barriers and found possible solutions to resolve them or found alternative ways around them.

If you scored 9 or 10, brilliant! You are in the right place. Success is getting closer and will definitely be in your grasp.

Remember to keep your TSB high. It's your life, you are in control, there is nothing life can throw at you that is bigger than you. Failure only occurs when you give up trying, all other outcomes and experiences are just feedback for you to work with and learn from.

## Katrina's Story

Katrina was dissatisfied with her life in general and felt trapped in a loveless marriage. Her husband did not look after her; he lacked ambition and displayed violent tendencies. She was reduced to cleaning toilets to make ends meet. Her future did not seem very bright.

Until one day she made a decision and finally broke free. It was both a relief and a shock. What was she to do now? She didn't even know who she was!

Katrina decided to start meeting new people; she started networking and discovered she liked talking to people. She shared her experiences and people listened. She also found that she could help others by talking through their problems and challenges with them. And so began her change journey of self-development.

Today, Katrina runs her own successful business helping others change. She is a qualified coach and is highly sought after in the corporate world, where she gives talks on leadership and regularly speaks at events championing the cause of women in business.

An amazing transformation!

## Doing, Doing, Done!

### Things to get done before you move on

- ✓ Who do you hang out with? Choose your circle carefully. Unhelpful beliefs can be infectious. Only when you are in your fresh new thinking mode can you spot them. **Check** ☐

- ✓ Have a good long hard look at all your connections, to identify the Sappers and Zappers. You know who they are deep down. Trust your gut instincts. **Check** ☐

- ✓ Let's play Ditch, Keep or Sound Out! Leave no stone unturned, this is your future at stake. No matter how painful, it's got to be done. You will feel re-energised. **Check** ☐

- ✓ Check your commitment level. Is it where it needs to be? If not, what's holding you back? Without full commitment you won't make the full journey. **Check** ☐

- ✓ REFLECTION: Find a quiet place where you won't be disturbed. Spend at least 20 minutes reflecting on what you did in this chapter. Ask yourself what did I learn from this? **Check** ☐

# CHAPTER 6: The Perfect Refinement

*"An ounce of practice is worth more than tons of preaching."*

Mahatma Gandhi

*"Practice as if you are the worst, perform as if you are the best."*

Anon

We already know that new habits are formed by repetition and old habits are eliminated by reduction and replacement, so it will come as no surprise that you will need to refine, refine, refine.

A phrase that I want you to lock in from my friend and highly successful self-improvement guru, Peter Thompson, is *"Perfect Practise Makes Perfect"*.

Let's unpick the key meaning of that, because it is important that you see it is different from what you might have previously heard, which is "Practice Makes Perfect".

What's important here is that it's true to say that the more you practise something, the better you get at it, but what happens if the way you have set up the practise is not perfect? You may be practising it in the wrong way, so although you will get better at something, it may not be what you really want.

What I am saying here is the routines, methods and situations that you use to practise being the New You are just as important as the practise itself.

Let's consider for example that you have decided the New You is going to be more upbeat and optimistic. You decide you are going to practise being more like this when you are out and you choose to use the situation of the pub/bar you visit twice a week with friends. If those friends generally spends their evenings at the pub bemoaning the economy, complaining about the government/council, or generally talking doom and gloom about world events or poverty (which happens to be common pastime in many drinking establishments), then it is unlikely that your practise will be very successful. Your intent and commitment to practise is commendable, but the planning was not perfect, hence your self-belief and confidence may take an early knock.

Make sure you give yourself the best chance to succeed, by choosing carefully.

## A Picture Speaks a Thousand Words

I now want to turn our attention to your image.

"What's all this about image?" I hear your inner critic muttering, "I'll skip this chapter…"

Well you know how to deal with that don't you!

Okay, so here's the thing, how you feel inside is significantly influenced by your perception of how you look on the outside. The previous 'you' had a particular look or image that has become aligned with that old you.

The New You deserves a change, a refresh, and what I have in mind for you is a bit of a makeover.

Consider this, if the New You were "beamed" (in a Star Trek sort of way) into a new town hundreds of miles away, into a new house, waiting for you to start a new life, what would the New You choose to wear? How would you have your hair? And if you wear make-up, how would you choose to wear it? What style of shoes would you wear? Etc.

Bear in mind, nobody would have any previous knowledge of you or how you used to look, so there would be no raised eyebrows! In other words how would you describe the style of the New You, what **message** does it send about the New You?

So come on, write a few ideas down in your journal.

Close your eyes, visualise yourself wearing those clothes, make-up, having that look. Notice what it feels like looking like that, visualise yourself in different scenarios: at home, casual, formal, at work, social. There's a real feel of the New You. What colours are you

THE Book on Personal Transformation

wearing? (Remember, you know how to visualise from the previous chapter.)

Now take your journal or piece of blank paper, and write down "My new image" across the top. Write down all the words that you can think of to describe the image you just visualised, single words if you like, colours, types of clothes, style descriptors. Include words about the image they portray. Keep going until you have covered every situation and every item of clothing and jewellery, make up, accessories, shoes, bag, hats, hairstyle etc., etc.

Congratulations! You have just created your master shopping list.

I want you to consider how you are going to keep this style constant - remember this is the New You. I don't want you to put on your new image to go out and then put on your old image again when you come home. So make sure you know how the New You will look when you're out and when you're at home, this will speed up the time it takes the New You to become the norm.

Remember, refine, refine, refine - every time you go out, take a look in the mirror, check how you look, and make sure the reflection exactly matches the image of the New You.

What about the way you speak? There may be nothing wrong with the way you speak and that's fine, but what if you feel it does not entirely match the New You? It is possible to change this too. Think about how some people choose to lose a regional accent. There's nothing wrong with a regional accent, but this is about exercising our free will and the right to choose. A search on the Internet will soon provide many options for elocution and speech training if that is what you want to do.

I want you to remember you deserve this, the New You, a new dawn, a new life, look good feel good, leave nothing to chance.

There are countless examples in today's world where people reinvent their look. A classic one here in the UK is Carol Vorderman. For many years she appeared on a TV show word game program, called 'Countdown', where she selected random letters contestants used to make words from and she also demonstrated clever mathematics skills using random numbers.

She was probably best described as a wholesome "girl next door", "butter wouldn't melt in her mouth" kind of girl with a brain. This was the image she portrayed for many years. She dressed conservatively and wore little makeup.

One day, out of the blue, the programmers decided to give the show a makeover and she was sacked. She has since revealed that she was devastated and initially thought her entire world would collapse.

However, if you were to Google her today you would find that she has completely reinvented herself; in fact the transformation is startling. She is now often described as a bit of a vamp, big hair, bold makeup, tight jeans or dresses and a vivacious, outgoing personality. It's hard to believe she is the same person - well she is the same person, just a new version of herself.

Being authentic is key, deep down inside it's still you; it's just that this part of you has never had a chance to come out before.

Refer back to your character and values lists, where did those preferences come from? They came from you. You were drawn to them from something inside you that either aligned with or desired them, you didn't make that up, it's real, and it's part of you.

I call it your **'Internal Resonance'**. We all have it, but often we don't tune into it or just ignore it.

If you have never considered what style is or how to create it, I suggest you buy some magazines. There are plenty to choose from for either sex, (UK examples for women might be: Elle, Vogue, Grazia, Harper's Bazaar, Cosmopolitan, etc., and for men: GQ, Tatler, Esquire, etc., and Google will offer plenty of options). Go and buy a few, have a look through them, see how others look, notice what styles resonate with you, and what styles could you see the New You wearing. Pick and mix if you want, if you see different items you like blend them together. Whatever you do, make sure you pay attention to your initial gut feeling, as I can guarantee your inner critic will be working overtime, wittering on about "Ooh that won't suit you" or "That's not really you, is it?" or "People will laugh at you if you wear that".

Well, you know how to deal with that don't you.

Next, armed with your new ideas (and maybe even a few pictures cut from the magazines), visit a good department store. Explain that you are looking for a 'New Look', they will normally be very helpful supplying options that fit with your ideas and descriptions and they may also provide you with some useful independent feedback. (They will of course also try to sell to you!)

This applies to both male and female departments.

Remember... you are not obliged to buy, even if they have helped you. You could use your initial shopping trip simply to get a feel of how things will look on you. Be confident and assertive, say "Thanks very much, I am still considering my options and want to look at some other stores first".

You can of course come back and buy their clothes once you have reflected and you are also free to shop around for equivalent items at lower priced stores, if budget is a restriction.

## Michael's Story

Michael had what most people would call a comfortable and stable upbringing. He grew up in a semi-detached house in Stroud, a nice town in Gloucestershire, with his mum, dad and two sisters. He cruised through school, achieving average grades and not really standing out in any way, good or bad.

After leaving school, Michael had a number of jobs, but nothing that really excited him, and when he turned 18 he found a job and moved to London.

He was very impressionable and soon began to mix with people who held anti-capitalist and anti-establishment views, which seemed to resonate with him. In fact he became so obsessed with them that within six months he had lost his job and was living in a large house that had been taken over as a 'free squat'.

He became bitter and negative about everything, drug use crept in and his health began to suffer. His family was cut out of his life, because they represented everything he was fighting against. He had no friends outside of his like-minded companions. He was scruffy, under nourished, bitter and argumentative.

He was far from happy; occasionally he would catch himself wishing for a different life, but he soon snapped back when he mixed with his companions.

That was until the day he had a weird experience. He found himself looking back at himself from afar, as if he was another person looking in.

What he saw shocked him to his core. "How had this happened?" he asked himself. This was not the future he had in mind when he came to London. And in that moment, a transition occurred. He made himself a promise that he would change. And so began his transformation journey.

He realised that for any lasting change to occur, he had to break out from the group he was mixing with, so one day he left the squat and never went back.

He moved across London and found a shelter group for the homeless, which allowed him to clean himself up. He ate a better diet and kicked the drugs habit.

He eventually got a job and found he really enjoyed fitness, so he trained hard himself. After a while he asked to join the staff in the local gym and they agreed. From there he worked his way up to lead instructor.

He is now very contented, has a healthy lifestyle, and has rebuilt his relationships with his family. Michael learned that although you can have bad personal transitions, you can recover by starting a positive transition.

### Doing, Doing, Done!

### Things to get done before you move on

- ✓ Practise makes perfect, but is your practise perfect? Choose wisely, reduce the risk of perceived failure and increase your chances of success. **Check** ☐

- ✓ A picture speaks a thousand words, so does your image! Ensure that the "looking" is aligned with the "doing", congruence is key. **Check** ☐

- ✓ Create your very own "Beam me down Scotty" moment. Be as free and creative as you can, it's your new life, your New You. **Check** ☐

- ✓ Reach inside and feel for your 'internal resonance'. Notice what really connects with you. Keep the 'critic' under control. **Check** ☐

- ✓ Launch your very own 'style-a-thon'. Get out there, try stuff on, mix and match, have some fun, be creative. Get in touch with how your new look feels and refine it. **Check** ☐

- ✓ REFLECTION: Find a quiet place where you won't be disturbed. Spend at least 20 minutes reflecting on what you did in this chapter. Ask yourself what did I learn from this? **Check** ☐

# CHAPTER 7: Onwards and Upwards

*"Success in life is a matter not so much of talent or opportunity as of concentration and perseverance."*

C. W. Wendte

Well done! I am very proud of you! I am assuming that now you have reached this point you are well on the way to permanently becoming the New You.

Remember, this is not a quick fix, it's a journey to the New You. I really want you to stay the distance and as with all the best laid plans, life can sometimes get in the way. So I have some tips that I know will help you stay the distance and truly become the New You.

**Tip #1 - Set yourself some goals and write them down.**

Remember, the world is your oyster, don't hold back. Life goals are really important, they keep us motivated and heading in a forward direction.

I recommend you set yourself some short-term, medium-term and long-term goals. Ensure they are positively phrased and aligned with the New You.

Keep them somewhere close where you can easily pull them out and review them regularly.

Here's my 5 step process for goal success:

1. Use the LMS sequence (Long, Medium, Short)
   Start with your long-term goal, write it down. Now consider what goals would be required in the medium term to make the long-term goals possible. Next decide what goals you would need to achieve in the short term in order to meet your medium-term goals.

2. Give them the STEAM format check, do they pass?
   This means you need to drill down into more specific detail.
   S is for Specific, exactly what are you referring to?
   T is for Timeframe, exactly when will this be done?

E is for Exciting, does this motivate you enough?
A is for Actionable, what actually needs to be done by whom?
M is for Measurable, how will you know when you have achieved it?

3. Make the Outcomes Well Formed
   Well-formed outcomes are essential to success. What will actually be different as a result of achieving this goal? How will you know? What will you see? What will you hear? What will you smell?

4. Review Regularly
   Set up a regular review process, fix it into your schedule. Don't just leave it to chance; build it in to your routine.

5. Be Flexible
   Yes, things won't go according to plan. Don't beat yourself up, it happens. Keep your motivation up and reschedule when things happen that are outside your control or unexpected events occur. On the other hand, don't let yourself get away with procrastination! Yes, you will know when it is.

## Tip #2 - Adopt a Positive Success Mindset PSM™

A positive success mindset is a very powerful way of keeping you moving forward when progress seems to be slow or setbacks feel like road blocks.

It's got nothing to do with just adopting a happy, smiley, "everything will be fine" attitude, but is a way of staying focused and attached to your bigger goal and tracking progress to stay motivated.

## BONUS #4

My fourth special bonus for you is a whole extra bonus chapter called **"How to Develop PSM™"**

This information is only normally available to my fee-paying personal coaching clients, but I have decided to give this to you as a special Thank You for buying my book.

# THE Book on Personal Transformation

You can access this valuable extra chapter online at **www.nowtransform.com**, just type the address into your browser's address field and then click on the **Bonus #4** button when you reach the website.

## Tip #3 – Maintain a Healthy Lifestyle

A healthy body supports a healthy mind. What do I mean by that?

Well our mind and body are in fact one integrated system and it stands to reason that if a significant part of that system is not operating at an optimum level, then it will impact the rest of the system. Carrying a little too much weight, combined with muscles that are rarely exercised, leaves the body and the mind sluggish. If you want to be on the top of your game, able to think clearly, respond to challenges and stay fresh, bright and motivated, you need to take care of your body. So what can you do?

Well, I'm not suggesting you become a fitness fanatic, but I am suggesting you take a good, hard, honest look at the amount of exercise that you do. Most of us have fallen into a sedentary lifestyle, driven by technology and a culture of immediacy.

See if you can change your routine - maybe use public transport instead of your car occasionally, and get off one stop earlier and walk the last section. Use the stairs instead of the lift wherever you can - you'll be amazed by how much better you'll feel after a few weeks and also how much more energy you will have.

Alternatively you could take up cycling; it's healthy and has other advantages like beating the traffic queues.

## Tip #4 – Change your Diet

It's important here to stress that I am not advocating you go on a 'diet' and become obsessed with counting calories. Far from it - when I say diet, I am referring to the range and type of food you eat regularly.

It is possible to make some simple changes that will have significant effects on your health and well-being. For example, wherever you have a choice, make a conscious choice to choose the healthier option, even if you are grabbing lunch on the go, a wrap, small salad and water is far better than that cheese and pickle sandwich, bag of crisps and can of cola! Or worse still, hot pie and chips. You don't need to become obsessive and you can still have the 'works' when you go out for a special meal, just change the choices you make day to day.

I suggest you reduce your intake of fried foods, bread and potatoes, and switch to wholegrain breads. Eat frequent small meals, rather than large full plates at the end of the day. Also withdraw your membership from the "Clear the Plate Club". Often our parents and society have conditioned us to think it is good to clear the plate, unfortunately they are wrong. Get back in touch with your body, it will TELL you when you have had enough food. Notice the signals/feelings and then stop, regardless of how much is left. Keep your alcohol intake to around the recommended guidelines; it's an often-forgotten high supplier of calories.

Adopting these eating habits, along with an increase in exercise will give you boundless energy and make you feel great.

Remember, I'm not advocating a strict diet, just suggesting you make small changes to the choices you make and if you go out for a celebration and overindulge - great, don't beat yourself up, it's ok once in a while, life is for living, and you still need to enjoy yourself. Just go back to making your sensible choices the next day.

**Tip #5 – Maintain a Healthy Mind**

By that I mean give your mind a chance to be in the best state possible to help you achieve your goals.

One of the best ways I know to do that is to practise 'light meditation' on a daily basis.

It is something I do daily, as it really helps to maintain focus and get things done. I suggest the best time of day to do this is first thing in the morning - you only need 15 – 20 minutes.

Here is a simple method you can follow to get started.

# THE Book on Personal Transformation

Find a quiet space where you won't be disturbed. Sit in a chair with your back upright and knees bent at right angles. (You could also sit cross legged on the floor if that would be more appropriate for you).

Place your hands on your knees (palms up) and let your forearms rest lightly on the top of your thighs, elbows bent at 90°.

Now close your eyes and take a few slow deep breaths. Breathe in through your mouth and out through your nose. Keep breathing in through your mouth and out through your nose. Begin to notice the sound of the air rushing through your nostrils, and try and notice the tiny changes in the sounds.

While you are continuing to listen, begin to relax your body. Start by focusing on the top of your head, notice you can relax it, and then slowly bring your attention down to the tops of your shoulders. Let them release and relax, still listening to the sound of the air rushing through your nostrils. Continue to move your attention slowly down your body, at each step taking time to relax that part even further, until you get all the way down to the tips of your toes.

Now you are fully relaxed, focus back in on your breathing. Focus all your thoughts on this; use your 'mind's eye' to look down onto your nose from an imaginary point in the centre of your head. Imagine you can see the air flowing through your nostrils. Keep this focus and allow your mind to become totally still, no thoughts at all other than the sound of the air in your nose. If a thought pops into your head (which it will), just acknowledge it and let it go. Imagine the thought is a twig, which you throw into a stream and watch it float away, and just refocus back on your breathing and notice the stillness of no thoughts.

Do this for about 15 – 20 minutes. You will notice your breathing will change and will become very light and shallow, and you will experience a sensation of calm and peace, a feeling of oneness.

When ready, slowly bring yourself back into the room and gently open your eyes.

Your day will now be more focused and effective.

## Tip #6 – Visualise your Success

My sixth tip is to spend about 10 minutes a day visualising your success.

You can do this whenever you wish. My suggestion is to do this twice a day. Once when you wake and again just before you go to sleep.

Use the meditation technique described in Tip #5 to relax yourself and then when your mind is quiet, visualise the things you want to achieve. Visualise short-term goals as well as your long-term goals. If it's a short-term goal and you do this in the morning then visualise yourself successfully achieving the things you want to achieve today. If in the evening, visualise yourself successfully achieving the things you want to achieve the following day.

Now I just want to expand a little on what mean by 'visualise'. I know not everyone uses their visual channel as their primary sense, but we all have the ability to imagine something, it's a bit like a day dream. Well that's exactly what visualisation is.

The key to successful visualisation is to visualise it from your own perspective (i.e. the first person) and invoke as many senses as possible.

I want you to FEEL it, SEE it, SMELL it, HEAR it, and make the experience in your mind as REAL as possible.

Another term used, which I mentioned briefly in Chapter 3, is mental rehearsal - when we rehearse something it means we are practising it over and over again until we get it perfect.

For example, let's imagine one of your short-term goals is to respond to people with a more positive approach and engage people in conversation rather than wait for them to speak to you.

You already know where you are likely to meet people during your day - on the bus, in the paper shop, on the train, in the office/workplace. So relax and start your daydream. See yourself enter the paper shop, see and hear yourself say the things you want the New You to say, imagine the response you might get from someone. Then play that scene over again, modify it slightly, hear yourself saying the words differently, how loud, what emphasis, how is your body language, eye contact. Run this over and over again until you feel everything is just how you would want it to be, for the mission to be classed as a success (against your criteria).

You have just rehearsed and by doing so, everything you have done has been burnt into your unconscious memory as an experience. Remember this part of your unconscious does not distinguish between imagined experience and real experience. This means that when you arrive at the paper shop tomorrow, your unconscious will remember, "Ah, I've been here before. This is where we engage in a positive conversation with people", and before you realise it, you have just spoken the words out loud and the conversation has taken place, either the same as or in a very similar way to how you imagined (rehearsed) it. RESULT! A successful outcome. It is unlikely to be the same word for word, because you cannot know exactly how others will reply, but the goal was not to predict exactly what would happen (that's called clairvoyance!), but to prime you to achieve a successful outcome, which in this case was to engage people in conversation in a positive manner.

Apply the same process for your long-term goals. It does not matter how far away from your current reality they are, take yourself to that place and point in time, imagine you have achieved a particular success, run it over and over, tweaking it each time, making it perfect. Bask in the amazing feelings of achievement. It's real, it's happened, this is you - touch it, feel it, make it bright and bold, and not only will your unconscious be primed and aligned, but you will also be sending out vibrations into the universe, sowing the seeds of the future and increasing the probability that it will come to fruition over time and with focused effort from you.

**Tip #7 – Programme your unconscious daily**

This is best done as you are waking. Your unconscious mind is totally subservient, it will obey whatever it believes you want or are. The biggest problem we face is our conscious mind, as this plays the role of gate keeper to our unconscious. Most of the time it filters things out, in order to protect the unconscious. But, the conscious mind goes to sleep when YOU are sleeping. The unconscious mind never sleeps, it is fully functioning 24/7, otherwise your body would just stop.

This means that when you are just waking up, the conscious mind is also only just waking up and therefore this is the best time to get easier access to your unconscious, the best time to do some subtle programming.

There are three things I recommend you do:

1. Programme your PURPOSE for the day
2. Programme how you want to BE today
3. Programme your SELF-BELIEF and SELF-ESTEEM for today.

1. Programme your PURPOSE for today.

To start this exercise you obviously need to have in mind what your purpose is for today. Initially this may sound a little weird, as we normally talk about purpose as a big-picture, life-goal kind of thing, but when you think about it we also have a mini purpose (or maybe several) every day, depending on what we are planning to do that day.

Let's say you want to have a positive impact on people today.

You would say in your head, using your inner supporter voice, something like this: "Thank you unconscious for helping me. My purpose today is to leave those I meet feeling glad they met me. Please help me achieve this." Say it over a few times.

You do not need to be more specific, your unconscious knows what this means and, due to its subservient nature, will set about making this come true. You will not notice it at the time, but at the end of the day, look back and I guarantee you will be pleased with the results.

2. Programme how you want to BE today

Again, this is to be done by speaking directly to your unconscious and is best done at the same time as programming your purpose.

Say something like this "Unconscious, today I want to be engaging and friendly. Please ensure I am engaging and friendly. Thank you." Again, say it over a few times, and again you do not need to be more specific, your unconscious will know what to do.

3. Programme your SELF-BELIEF and SELF-ESTEEM for today

This process takes the form of affirmations rather than requests. These will reinforce the changes you are making. It is very important to ensure that you state these in the present tense, as if they are already true and I'll explain why.

Remember what we learnt about your unconscious - it holds your beliefs. Beliefs are built over a period of time, often as a result of prolonged reinforcement. The more your unconscious hears something over time, the more it will start to believe it. When your unconscious believes something about you, it will then slavishly ensure that your behaviours align with that belief. It cannot and does not make any judgements about you; all those are done by your conscious mind.

Not surprisingly, your inner critic will spring into action and try to counter them with "Oh no you're not" statements, deal with these in the way you learnt in Chapter 4.

Affirmations can be said in your head but work best if they are spoken out loud and even better if you can say them while looking in a mirror.

Refer to your characteristics list and select the top three.

Say these out loud:

1. I am "insert characteristic 1"
2. I am "insert characteristic 2"
3. I am "insert characteristic 3"
4. I am a SUCCESSFUL person
5. I completely RESPECT me
6. I totally TRUST myself
7. I really LIKE who I am
8. I am a CONFIDENT person

Say these over about 10 times.

Remember, we know they are not all true yet, but it's our unconscious we are talking to.

So, here's the schedule:

Do these three sets of exercises every single day for at least 30 days, with no breaks. If you have a day when you just cannot do them, you will need to reset the counter back to zero and start again.

Trust me, you will be amazed and delighted with the results you achieve.

After you have completed this for one set of characteristics, start again with a new set, make it a way of life.

### Tip #8 – Relax, Have Fun

Relax, have fun and don't take things too seriously. Detach yourself from the outcome. If you spend all your time worrying that it's not happening or it won't happen, guess what, it probably won't happen!

I'm sure you have heard many stories of couples that are trying to have a baby but are unable to fall pregnant. Tests reveal that there is no medical reason on either side as to why this is happening. The couple become very stressed and obsessed with trying every possible remedy they can find, from timing when they make love to the exact minute of her bio rhythms, to eating blueberry jam, to filling the room full of wild flowers. They are completely 'attached to the outcome', but nothing works. They become even more stressed and finally resign themselves to the fact that it's not going to happen for them.

They take a holiday and lo and behold, after they return home she discovers she has fallen pregnant and the dates suggest it happened while they were on holiday. Why? Because they were relaxed and detached from the outcome.

So, do the stuff, have fun in the process, and don't forget to relax.

**BONUS #5**

My fifth and final Special Bonus for you is some rocket fuel for your mind.

I have recorded a unique audio track especially for the readers of my book, designed to programme your mind for success and boost your motivation levels sky high. After listening to this bonus audio, you will know you can take on the world and will be buzzing with energy and determination, massively increasing your chance of success.

Find somewhere quiet where you will not be disturbed for about 10 minutes and prepare for blast off. It is best listened to with headphones or ear pods, but definitely NOT when driving!

If you have been following the steps of the book you will have already logged on to the bonus site and know where to find this priceless bonus, but just in case you have not, then go to **www.nowtransform.com** and click on **Bonus #5**

For those of you that really want to guarantee success you can always choose to be coached by me, just visit **www.coach-my-success.com**

## LIFE HAPPENS

Lastly I want to deal with the reality of life.

Things will go wrong and you will have unexpected setbacks - that's life and it's the same for all of us.

The most important advice I can give you is to 'change the way you think about problems'.

What do I mean by that?

"It's not the problems that affect our success, but the way we THINK about them."

Ask any successful person how they cope when things go wrong (which happens to everyone), and they will tell you it's all to do with how they view the situation.

Take for example Simon Cowell, the hugely successful talent show guru. Right now he is enjoying enormous international success, along with all the trappings of wealth that go with it. But it was not always like that.

When Simon first started out in business, he built up an extremely successful record label and was living a life of luxury when in 1989 at the age of 30, everything crashed down around him. His business went bust leaving huge debts. Simon had to relinquish all his luxuries, big house, flash cars, etc., and at the age of 30, move back in with his mum. For some people, this humiliation may have been crushing and left them believing they were a failure, but not Cowell. He viewed it differently, as a minor setback. The key thing is that he did not view it as a PERSONAL failure. It was just one of those things that happens in business and within a year he had another successful record label up and running, which eventually lead to his involvement with BMG-Sony, and the rest, as they say, is history.

So when things don't go right, learn from them, don't take it personally, it's only the thing that failed, not you. Get up, dust yourself down, regroup and move forward.

# THE FINAL WORD

So that's it, you are now well on your way. I wish you luck.

Remember you are special and unique; nothing is greater than your ability to deal with it (whatever 'it' may be).

You are in control of you, no one else. What you focus on is what you get.

Relax and enjoy the ride.

*"Whether you think you can or you think you can't, you're probably right"*
Henry Ford

*"A man is but the product of his thoughts what he thinks, he becomes"*
Mahatma Gandhi


Good Luck,

I wish you Health, Wealth and Happiness.

And remember

Live Well
Laugh Often,
Love each Other
and above all, Be True to the Real You

Your Coach

Peter

# A Note from the Author

I first became interested in personal development when I attended training courses as a young manager in a big corporation. I became fascinated by the world of psychology and human behaviour and the art of success. As a leader and coach I love helping others achieve their goals and success.

As I began to achieve personal success, I started to look more closely at what I was doing to create this success. This gave me great insights into the power of the mind, personal responsibility and making choices; I realised that we create our own experiences of every situation and can therefore affect and control the impact on ourselves and the results we achieve.

This was put to the test when my first marriage broke down while my children were in their formative years. They moved away with my ex-wife and I found myself living in a rented room with few possessions – a huge change from having a nice home and 'normal' family life. I chose not to let the circumstances control how I felt or influence my approach on life and as a result I found more positive things happened for me, including a new marriage and great relationships with my children.

More recently I found myself disillusioned with the politics of the corporate world and decided to leave and branch out on my own. It was the best decision I have ever made, but it also required me to go through some reinvention myself. I now spend my time helping others reinvent themselves, transform their lives, reach their goals and achieve success, while simultaneously continuing my own personal development and continuous learning in the art of success.

Along the way I have had the privilege to meet some wonderful people who have achieved amazing and inspiring personal transformations.

I am now a Personal Transformation Coach, writer, speaker and businessman, living on purpose with a clear direction and being true to the real me. Life is good.

Made in the USA
Charleston, SC
24 November 2012